"This book is a son[g] [to] the Northwest's iconic music scene. From jazz on Jackson to Black Belt Eagle Scout and all the badasses in between, you will swing, mosh, headbang, shimmy, and sway your way through the music, places, and people that define the sound of Seattle. Buckle up, bitches!"
MEGAN JASPER, SUB POP RECORDS CEO

"Jake and Eva have crafted a fun and breezy romp through some of the most important spots of Northwest music history. The songs referenced should be required listening for anyone with a love of Northwest music, and in my book—and in this one—these locations are shrines to an important cultural history past and present, which this book lovingly details."
CHARLES R. CROSS, *NEW YORK TIMES*–BESTSELLING AUTHOR

"Thank you, Eva and Jake, for writing this informative and heartfelt book about a subject close to my heart, the music culture of the Pacific Northwest."
MATT CAMERON, ROCK & ROLL HALL OF FAME DRUMMER

"Jake and Eva are so ingrained in this city's musical landscape that I couldn't wait to read this book! They put together bite-sized journals of our city's music history in a way that I've never seen. There's a lot of books about Seattle music but none like this!"
MARCO COLLINS, LEGENDARY SEATTLE RADIO DJ (FEATURED IN THE ROCK & ROLL HALL OF FAME)

Printed in China

SASQUATCH BOOKS
with colophon is a
registered trademark of
Penguin Random House LLC

28 27 26 25 24
9 8 7 6 5 4 3 2 1

Editor: Jen Worick
Production editor: Isabella Hardie
Design: Alison Keefe

Library of Congress Cataloging-in-
Publication Data

Names: Walker, Eva, author. |
   Uitti, Jacob, author.
Title: The sound of Seattle : 101
   songs that shaped a city / Eva
   Walker, Jacob Uitti.
Identifiers:
   LCCN 2023044474 (print) |
   LCCN 2023044475 (ebook) |
   ISBN 9781632175144 (paperback)
   | ISBN 9781632175151 (ebook)
Subjects: LCSH: Popular
   music--Washington (State)--
   Seattle--History and
   criticism. | Musicians--
   Washington (State)--Seattle.
Classification: LCC ML3477.8.S33
   W35 2024 (print) | LCC
   ML3477.8.S33
   (ebook) | DDC
   781.6409797/772--dc23
   eng/20230922
LC record available at https://lccn
   loc.gov/2023044474
LC ebook record available at
   https://lccn.loc.gov/2023044475

ISBN: 978-1-63217-514-4

Sasquatch Books
1325 Fourth Avenue, Suite 1025
Seattle, WA 98101

SasquatchBooks.com

101 SONGS
THAT SHAPED A CITY

Eva Walker
Jacob Uitti

 SASQUATCH BOOKS | SEATTLE

CONTENTS

FOREWORD

The Seattle music scene goes back many decades, but my introduction was when my parents bought me a $100 guitar in 1978. After taking some lessons, I joined the band Warrior when I was at Eckstein Middle School in seventh grade. The band consisted of Rick Friel on bass, Danny Newcomb on guitar, and Chris Friel on drums. After joining Warrior, we immediately took rehearsing seriously and practiced—really loudly—at the Friel house in a room just off the garage. We would spend the next five years rehearsing five days a week for at least three hours a day and developed a punk-meets-metal sound.

My very first show was a birthday party for our friend Jenny at her house in 1979. We played a few originals and covered the Beatles' "Daytripper." In 1981 we asked a singer named Rob "Berko" Webber, who I'd known since kindergarten, to join the band. Around this time, we changed our name to Shadow and played all over the Northwest at places like Lake Hills Roller Rink, Fremont Baptist Church, the Mountaineers Club, Port Orchard Armory, Bremerton High School, Polish Hall, and the Norway Center. We even got to play at the Moore Theatre a couple times for Headbangers Ball.

In 1983, *The Rocket* magazine ranked us the #4 "Best Local Band" along with 10 Minute Warning (#3),

the Allies (#2), and Queensrÿche and Culprit (tied for #1). It was crazy because we were all only about seventeen years old at that time. Like our friends in Overlord, Rids, and TKO, we had to play in a city that wasn't supportive of all-ages rock shows. The silly and futile Teenage Dance Ordinance forbade us and others who were under twenty-one from playing at bars—important places to develop at the time. This gave Shadow and other bands the "DIY attitude" and motivation to put on our own shows, put up our own flyers, and record our own demos and records.

In 1987, Danny and Rob left the band, so Shadow became a three-piece with Rick, Chris, and me. About a year later our friend Duff McKagan from 10 Minute Warning stopped by the Friel house and told us he was moving to Los Angeles. When we saw things happening for Duff in Guns N' Roses a few years later, we decided to move down there to try and "make it." However, we only lasted about a year before I got sick with Crohn's disease, and I decided to move home and quit music.

Then I got a call from Stone Gossard and things changed . . .

Bottom line, I grew up in the Seattle music scene and it sure was fun. Music was everything to me back then, just as it is now.

—*Mike McCready*

▲ Marquee at the Showbox on 1st Avenue, Seattle, 1940

INTRODUCTION

The first time I saw my wife, she was onstage singing. I didn't know her band at the time. But I was suddenly glad to be at Tractor Tavern, invited to write about the Friday night rock bill. I walked to the back of the room to get a seat, but there were only two stools open among the big audience and piles of belongings. I went to sit down when a stranger reached out. "That's the singer's mom's seat!"

Confused, I looked to the stage and saw the Black Tones: frontwoman Eva Walker, twin brother Cedric on drums, mother and sister backup singers. Quintessential rock music *and* a family band? They captivated the room to such a degree that their seats were being saved *while* they were performing. That's the power of music in Seattle. The art form is currency here.

In Seattle, music brings people together around a common love. In song. In authorship. Even in marriage. And after that night at the Tractor, Eva and I began to date. Today, we are married and, gratefully, the authors of this book too. *The Sound of Seattle* is our bow to music. We wouldn't be together without it.

In every neighborhood of the city, music pours out. From festivals to local radio stations, from practice rooms to live performances. The region has always been resonant that way. The sounds change but there is always regeneration and experimentation, even in tragedy. From the jazz of Ray Charles and croon of Bing Crosby (who once asked my Hollywood actress aunt, Betty Uitti, to marry him; she declined) to the rock of chart-topper Ayron Jones, Seattle music is eternal.

Indeed, people in Seattle grow up learning the city's music history as others elsewhere learn about local sports heroes. Kurt, Jimi, Quincy, the Heart sisters— these are our founding figures. The city touches all genres, from Grammy Award–winning classical recordings to Muzak, which used to be based here. And while we couldn't cover every band in these pages, we hope you will see important lineages, trends, and styles unfold, and cherish the diversity of the sounds.

Whether it sits at the epicenter of pop culture (as it did in the '90s) or takes the occasional backseat, the Emerald City always manages to move us.

—*Jake Uitti*

The
1940s
-50s

JAZZ AND JACKSON STREET

As the twentieth century's door opened, Seattle was increasingly defined by its industry. An outpost in the country's upper-left, it was the last stop for those on the Yukon Gold Rush, and it was also a major hub for the timber business. With both, of course, came nightlife.

Throughout its history, Seattle has been home to vaudeville performers and live musicians. As author Paul De Barros highlights in his comprehensive 1993 book, *Jackson Street After Hours*, the city's entertainment scene thrived early on, even if mainstream attention wasn't paid.

As early as 1918, Lillian Smith's acclaimed jazz band performed at Seattle's Washington Hall. In the following decades, the city became an important area for military and defense projects, thanks to its location on the map and the presence of Boeing. The city grew.

In 1962, Elvis and the World's Fair came, and in 1967 the region got its first sports team, the SuperSonics. Seattle was a hot spot. But prior, the city's jazz scene, which included locals (Ray Charles) and touring artists (Charlie Parker and Duke Ellington), bustled.

In 1948, a teenage Charles moved to Seattle from Florida.

Here, he wrote some of his first songs and got his first record deal, flying to L.A. to cut his first single. Then, a young Ernestine Anderson began to make a name for herself too. And local wunderkind Quincy Jones saw it all.

Eight years after Charles, future country star Willie Nelson moved some miles south of Seattle to Vancouver, Washington, where he worked at the radio station KVAN. There, he quietly cut his first single, "No Place for Me," in 1956 and wrote his future first hit, "Family Bible."

But back in the city, clubs like the Black and Tan were important to the fabric. And as De Barros notes, Jackson Street was at the center of the party. The writers thank newspapers like the *Northwest Enterprise* and historians like Esther Mumford for their coverage of it all back then.

At a time when most outlets ignored jazz, some kept as watchful an eye as they could. "For, in the face of these obstacles—being forced underground, harassed by the authorities, ignored by the press—Seattle jazz musicians have fared remarkably well," writes De Barros in his book.

Thank goodness for the artists' resolve. Seattle wouldn't be the same without it.

BING CROSBY

SINGLE: "WHITE CHRISTMAS"

RECORD: SONG HITS FROM HOLIDAY INN

RELEASED: 1942 | **RECORDED IN:** LOS ANGELES

PRODUCER: IRVING BERLIN | **LABEL:** DECCA

The region's original big-name
musician came up many decades before
"Nevermind" or "Purple Haze." Born in
Tacoma, Washington in 1903 and raised
in Spokane, Washington, Harry Lillis
"Bing" Crosby Jr. boasts the distinction
of being the first modern multimedia star
from the Northwest or otherwise.

Crosby, who began recording in 1931,
tallying 71 albums and 409 singles,
earned his biggest hit a decade later
when he performed the Irving Berlin holiday song "White Christmas" on a radio
broadcast on Christmas Day 1941, just
weeks after the attack on Pearl Harbor.
(Berlin's own son died on Christmas Day
in 1928.) Incidentally, the Seattle-born
Broadway star Carol Channing started her
iconic career in New York City also in
'41. Crosby's official studio recording
of the song, which took a mere eighteen
minutes to track and included the Ken

Darby Singers and John Scott Trotter and
His Orchestra, hit No. 1 on Halloween
1942, where it remained on the charts
for eleven weeks.

Today, the song is the world's bestselling single of all time (selling tens of millions of copies). With
a buttery-smooth voice that defines
"croon," Crosby's version of the classic Berlin number remains popular when-
ever snow falls around December 25.

THE SHOWBOX AT THE MARKET

1426 1ST AVENUE, SEATTLE

In Seattle, there are two concert venues known as the Showbox. But it's the one across the street from Pike Place Market that just might be the most important venue in the city.

There are bigger venues like the Paramount Theatre, with its ornate, cathedral-like interior design, and venues in historic neighborhoods, like Tractor Tavern in Ballard and Central Saloon in Pioneer Square, but the Showbox at the Market is the one that combines all the best features of a kickass venue to create one 1,150-person home. For bands, the Showbox at the Market is the place to play. It's large but unassuming, historic but not lavish. It's been host to local musicians like Macklemore & Ryan Lewis, Soundgarden, Death Cab for Cutie, and countless others. It's also been a stage for many national and international artists.

The venue is in the heart of downtown, separated by a block of cobblestone road from the Market, with its fish throws, bushels of brightly colored flowers, and busking up-and-coming artists. The Showbox at the Market's marquee is a must-see when you pass by in a car, cab, or pedal taxi. *Who's playing this week?* Many locals have taken a selfie under the display that might, for a night, show off names like Travis Thompson or Thunderpussy. It's a badge of honor as much as any advertisement.

Founded in 1939, the venue has been owned by AEG Live since 2007. In the years between it was used, among other things, as a comedy and supper club. Today the venue is so beloved that when there was a push to turn it into a forty-two-floor apartment tower in 2018, everyone in the city—from fans to artists to politicians—shouted the refrain "Save our Showbox," refusing to let it go. In 2019, the Showbox was granted landmark status by Seattle's Landmarks Preservation Board, and it continues to rock on.

RAY CHARLES

SINGLE: "CONFESSION BLUES"

RECORD: CONFESSION BLUES

RELEASED: 1949 | **RECORDED IN:** LOS ANGELES

PRODUCER: JACK LAUDERDALE | **LABEL:** DOWN BEAT

Born in 1930 in Georgia, Ray Charles grew up to become one of the most significant artists of the twentieth century. But it was in Seattle where he cut his teeth. Charles, who moved to the Emerald City from Florida by bus, began playing in the region's popular jazz joints and earned a name for himself. Soon, he started his McSon Trio (known erroneously also as "the Maxin Trio"). And it was with that band that Charles earned his first recording project.

In 1949, Charles and the group flew to Los Angeles to record their song "Confession Blues" with Down Beat. The tune is mellow by Charles's standards. It was also his first to ever chart on Billboard. The track, which features precise, staccato rhythm piano, twinkling keys, and guitar leads at various intervals, along with Charles's smooth yet somehow raspy voice, indicated a rising star. By the time he passed away in 2004, Charles boasted sixty-two solo albums.

One can only imagine now walking into a
Jackson Street nightclub and, through the cigarette smoke, spotting Charles at the piano,
backed by upright bass and guitar. Even with
clinking glasses everywhere, all the attention
is on the dynamo in dark sunglasses. Seattle
was so important to his artistic development
that his Oscar-winning biopic starring Jamie
Foxx highlights his time there, which includes
meeting an enthusiastic teenage Quincy Jones.

WASHINGTON HALL

153 14TH AVENUE, SEATTLE

Built in 1908, Washington Hall has been a staple in Seattle's Central District from day one. Just ten years later, the venue held the city's first-ever jazz performance, a 1918 fundraiser for the NAACP. The music that night came from Miss Lillian Smith's Jazz Band. To many, including local author Paul De Barros, that moment is considered the big bang for jazz in the city.

Not far from Washington Hall is South Jackson Street, where jazz in Seattle flourished. It's a history that De Barros covered in *Jackson Street After Hours*. That part of town also saw the birth of hip-hop in Seattle, as detailed in Daudi Abe's book, *Emerald Street: A History of Hip Hop in Seattle*. It was a fertile ground that De Barros called a "hub of . . . authentic Black jazz."

Over the years, Washington Hall has hosted many historical figures in music, including Billie Holiday, Cab Calloway, Duke Ellington, and Jimi Hendrix. Others since include influential punk acts of the 1980s, local hip-hop pioneers Emerald Street Boys, and even grunge bands like early groundbreakers 10 Minute Warning. Today, the building remains viable for artists to perform in and showcase new work.

In 2009, the Historic Seattle organization took over operations of the building, purchasing it with a grant from the Washington State Historical Society and 4Culture. This removed any possibility of demolition. Now, it's earned historical landmark status and will remain safe for years.

ERNESTINE ANDERSON

SINGLE: "THE SONG IS ENDED"

RECORD: HOT CARGO

RELEASED: 1958 | **RECORDED IN:** STOCKHOLM, SWEDEN

PRODUCER: BÖRJE EKBERG | **LABEL:** MERCURY RECORDS

Born in 1928 in Houston, Texas, Ernestine Anderson's family moved to Seattle in the 1940s when she was sixteen. There, she joined the impressive list of Garfield High School alumni, along with Quincy Jones and Ray Charles. Later, she recorded "The Song Is Ended" in Stockholm, Sweden, on what was likely a very cold afternoon in November 1956, just eight days before her (and her twin sister Josephine's) twenty-seventh birthday. Anderson was there while on tour, heading to the rest of Scandinavia next with trumpeter Rolf Ericson.

This song, although performed as a jazz number, is as much a blues story of lost love. From the gray winters of Seattle to the freezing winters of Stockholm, the four-time Grammy-nominated Anderson —who would later perform at both Carnegie Hall and the Kennedy Center among other prestigious venues, and sign

to Quincy Jones's Qwest Records in the
1990s—brings the Texas heat along with
a band of piping hot musicians to create
this jazz number.

In 2012, Anderson, who'd lived in
Seattle's Central District, was recognized when a housing project was named
in her honor. After she passed away
in 2016, the city also placed an hon-
orary street sign with her name along
South Jackson Street, between 20th
Avenue South and 23rd Avenue, right near
Ernestine Anderson Place housing.

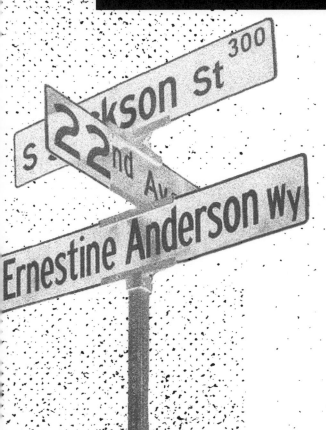

THE FABULOUS WAILERS

SINGLE: "TALL COOL ONE"

RECORD: THE FABULOUS WAILERS

RELEASED: 1959 | **RECORDED IN:** LAKEWOOD, WA; NEW YORK CITY

PRODUCER: CLARK GALEHOUSE | **LABEL:** GOLDEN CREST RECORDS

Formed in Tacoma in 1958, the Fabulous Wailers were one of the region's founding fathers of rock. According to legend, the group, known first as the Nitecaps, was a favorite of a young guitar player in the area: Jimi Hendrix. But before Hendrix was shredding on "Foxy Lady," the Fabulous Wailers were writing and playing songs in their garage. Seattle was home to many important garage rock groups, from the Wailers to the Sonics, to Tom Thumb & the Casuals. And in Portland, other bands like the Kingsmen were following suit.

The Wailers' first hit was the saxophone-driven, brooding blues instrumental "Tall Cool One." First titled "Scotch on the Rocks," the group's label, Gold Crest Records, had them change it to a more family-friendly name. The song peaked at No. 36 on the Billboard Hot 100 charts and its success led to more recordings, including their self-titled debut LP. The group, which appeared on Dick Clark's *American Bandstand* television show, recorded a cover of Richard

Berry's classic "Louie Louie" in 1961, a song later made famous by the Portland band the Kingsmen. ("Louie Louie," once banned by the governor of Indiana in the '60s, has even become the unofficial rock song for Washington state. Go figure.) All in all, the Wailers released seven studio albums and their influence can still be heard in rock today.

The 1960s

TALKING FATE with MERRILEE RUSH

Merrilee Rush wouldn't have wanted to be in Seattle at any other time. The singer of the 1968 hit "Angel of the Morning," says the '60s, with acts like the Wailers, the Sonics, Tiny Tony, the Statics, the Playboys, the Dynamics, Nancy Claire, and Gale Harris, were glorious. Back then, the city was rich with what it still has now—bountiful radio stations; venues for everyone; and bands, bands, bands—but in the '60s, everything was just unique and starting to crackle.

"I think because we were isolated," says Rush. "We weren't influenced by the next-door neighbor. Seattle has its own region, its own thing."

Rush recalls venues like Parker's Ballroom, which opened in 1930 on Aurora, where acts could perform to hundreds of people, fostering a community and an exciting culture. It was a home to jazz in the '40s, rock in the '50s, and the experimental music of the '60s. And there were more, including teenage dancehalls from Seattle to Tacoma, and bars, theaters, and restaurants. On the airwaves, KJR was influential to the region, bringing the personalities of the local DJs to the songs. As was KZAM, a station so popular people bought new FM tuners to listen.

"Because those jocks were personality jocks," says Rush, "they gave our region our own personality. They were playing pop music, surfer music, but there was a character that came from those stations. They were cool, they were funny, they were hip."

Rush, growing up post-WWII, loved the radio, particularly listening to R & B. She'd come home from school, sit down by the dial, and listen. She'd flip through the lyrics printed in her *Hit Parader* magazine and sing along. In the R & B days of the early '60s, she'd buy records at the Little Record Mart on Madison. Later, Rush started her career in earnest when she joined her now-ex-husband's band, the Aztecs. From there, Rush formed Merrilee and Her Men.

"I'm just so lucky to have been where I was," she says, "because I was there when rock and roll happened in the mid-'50s. I was there with Elvis and Bill Haley and the Comets. They took swing into the rock era. It was just a wonderful time."

Rush's world changed when she got an opening slot on tour with Boise band Paul Revere & the Raiders. Hanging out in a Memphis studio at the end of the Raiders tour, Rush cut a demo. Her singing impressed the studio producer and a month later she was brought back to record more. During this time, she was shown the revolutionary "Angel of the Morning," written by Chip Taylor, author of "Wild Thing." And she dug in.

"As I'm reading the lyric," Rush says, "I'm thinking, 'Oh my god, people are going to want to hear this again and hear this lyric!' It hadn't been said that way before."

The song of female empowerment became a worldwide hit for her. From the early jazz in the '40s to the R & B beginnings of the '60s to the evolution of rock and pop music, Rush has seen so much happen in Seattle, and now she is part of its lore. And given Seattle's long history of loving rock music, it's no surprise Heart and later bands were able to thrive in the scene. "For it to evolve into

grunge, I can totally understand," Rush adds.

Perhaps more than any other
local star, Rush has witnessed
the city's evolution, from
teenage dance halls in the '60s,
with audience members like
the teenage Heart sisters, to
the Showbox and Paramount
today. But that hasn't changed
Rush's love for the region. For
some, familiarity breeds con-
tempt. But for Rush, it fosters
a love affair. "We're so lucky
to live here," Rush says. "I've
lived here all my life, born and
raised. I was meant to be here."

▲ Paul Revere and the Raiders promoting an album release, Seattle, 1967

LORETTA LYNN

SINGLE: "I'M A HONKY TONK GIRL"

RECORD: I'M A HONKY TONK GIRL

RELEASED: 1960 | **RECORDED IN:** LOS ANGELES

PRODUCER: DON GRASHEY | **LABEL:** ZERO

Few names in country music rival Loretta Lynn. The artist who wrote "The Pill" also happened to be a Pacific Northwesterner. Here, Lynn wrote what would become her debut single while living as a young homemaker in Washington. That song, "I'm a Honky Tonk Girl," was recorded in Los Angeles and released in the spring of 1960. Lynn and her then-husband promoted the song, which hit No. 14 on the Billboard Hot Country Songs chart, driving from radio station to radio station.

The tune about loss was inspired by a woman Lynn met in her travels in Washington. That woman told Lynn a sob story about losing everything. And Lynn wrote the lyrics in twenty minutes in her bathroom, using a $17 guitar that her husband bought her. She also wrote "Whispering Sea" in that same session. The man who helped pay for the L.A. recording also had a connection to the newly founded Zero Records, which would become Lynn's first label.

Born in Kentucky, the teenage Lynn married her husband Oliver in 1948 after knowing him for only a month. Together, they moved from the Bluegrass State to Custer, then known as a PNW logging town, when Lynn was seven months pregnant. In 1953, Lynn started to teach herself to play on the $17 guitar, fitting her lyrics to music. Shortly after, she started her first band, Loretta and the Trailblazers, playing Washington venues in Blaine, Custer, and elsewhere. She even won a talent contest in Tacoma hosted by country icon Buck Owens, originator of the Bakersfield, California country sound, who was also living in the PNW at the time.

DAVE LEWIS

SINGLE: "LITTLE GREEN THING"

RECORD: LITTLE GREEN THING

RELEASED: 1964 | **RECORDED IN:** SEATTLE

PRODUCER: JERRY DENNON | **LABEL:** A&M RECORDS

Born in Texas in 1938, musician Dave Lewis moved with his family to Bremerton, Washington, during World War II. Living in the racially segregated Sinclair Heights housing projects, Lewis's musical family consisted of his father, a guitarist who would sometimes give their young neighbor Quincy Jones music lessons, and mother, a piano player. Later, the family moved to Seattle, where Dave attended Garfield and Franklin high schools.

By the summer of 1956, his band had become one of the hottest acts in the region, which led to opening opportunities on tours across the Pacific Northwest and the chance to share stages with Roy Orbison, Little Richard, and Ray Charles. After a slew of successful local gigs, including an opportunity at the city's famed World's Fair, Lewis switched from piano to Hammond B-3 and

formed a new organ trio that
performed the local hit,
"Little Green Thing."
The song appeared
on the album of the
same name, released
via A&M Records
in 1964. On it,
Lewis, whose grand-
son D'Vonne is a local
drummer (see Industrial
Revelation on page 218),
makes the organ sound
like someone is rip-
ping its heart out.

THE
EDGEWATER
HOTEL

2411 ALASKAN WAY, SEATTLE

Beatles fans, you might want to sit down. Did you know there is a Fab Four–themed suite in Seattle's Edgewater Hotel where the band once stayed? The posh suite available to rent commemorates the famous Mop Tops' stay in 1964 at the height of Beatlemania.

These days, the hotel, located on a pier off Alaskan Way overlooking the city's sparkling Elliott Bay, bills itself as "Seattle's only over-water hotel." And they're right. The hotel, which was built in 1962 for the World's Fair in Seattle, boasts four stories, over 200 rooms, and once advertised that visitors could fish from their windows. The Beatles did just that when they visited (taking a photo while doing so). Other Rock & Roll Hall of Fame rock luminaries who've stayed there include Led Zeppelin, Neil Young, Kurt Cobain, and Black Sabbath. In fact, Robert

Plant, Jimmy Page, and the rest of the Zeppelin crew were banned from the facilities after poor behavior during the British-born band's second stay in the Emerald City.

Today, though room rates can be spendy, the views, fresh ocean air, rock and roll stories, and proximity to Pike Place Market make the price worth it. The place is unique, after all. Not long after the Edgewater (formerly the Edgewater Inn and originally the Camelot) was built, the city changed its zoning laws to make it illegal for hotels to be built on piers. So, while the building stands alone as a one-of-a-kind hotel in the city's landscape, it also remains a distinct, popular cultural attraction, a once-upon-a-time home to some of the biggest bands in history.

THE SONICS

SINGLE: "THE WITCH"

RECORD: !!!HERE ARE THE SONICS!!!

RELEASED: 1965 | **RECORDED IN:** SEATTLE

PRODUCER: BUCK ORMSBY, KENT MORRILL

LABEL: ETIQUETTE RECORDS

Before the Pacific Northwest encoun-
tered Bob Rule and the Lenny Wilkens
era, they saw the *band*, the Sonics, not
the since-stolen NBA team. Hailing from
Tacoma, the Sonics were formed in 1960
by Larry Parypa, whose brother Andy
later joined on bass. As members came
and went, the group eventually recruited
Bob Bennett, Gerry Roslie, and sax
player Rob Lind, all of whom previously
played together in another outfit called
the Searchers.

This newly solidified lineup began their
formal journey most notably when Roslie,
originally the Searchers' keyboardist,
began singing lead. The Sonics played in
myriad venues across the Northwest and
eventually signed to Etiquette Records
after being scouted by Buck Ormsby of
the Wailers. "The Witch" was the Sonics'
first single and a year later it was the

first track on their debut album, *!!!Here Are the Sonics!!!*, recorded in 1964— their first of five studio albums.

The Sonics' heavy garage rock and punk sound on "The Witch" is something of an antithesis to then-contemporary acts like the Beatles, with their neatly combed hair and ironed clothes. The Sonics' sound was more raw force than smoothness. Yet, in the end, "The Witch" is arguably as powerful as anything the Fab Four put out at the time.

JIMI HENDRIX

SINGLE: "PURPLE HAZE"

RECORD: ARE YOU EXPERIENCED

RELEASED: 1967 | **RECORDED IN:** LONDON

PRODUCER: CHAS CHANDLER | **LABEL:** TRACK RECORD

Jimi Hendrix was born in Seattle on November 27, 1942. And he was fifteen when he first picked up a guitar, a decision that would change the fate of music forever. With a solo career that spanned just three years before his death on September 18, 1970, Hendrix is nevertheless considered to be the greatest electric guitarist ever. In fact, the Rock & Roll Hall of Fame, which inducted Hendrix into its distinguished ranks in 1992, considers him the greatest instrumentalist in the history of rock music.

Early in his musical journey, Hendrix accompanied acts like the Isley Brothers, Little Richard, and Ike and Tina Turner as a backup player. Eventually, through a referral by Rolling Stones guitarist Keith Richards, he was connected with manager Chas Chandler, who soon began hiring members for a new band called the Jimi Hendrix Experience. For Hendrix's backup, Chandler recruited Noel Redding on bass and drummer Mitch Mitchell. The trio's debut album, *Are You Experienced* —released on May 12, 1967—was met with immediate commercial success.

The album, first released in the UK, includes hits like "Red House," "Manic Depression," and "Foxy Lady." The North American edition includes one of his biggest hits, "Purple Haze." That song opens with just two notes seesawing on Hendrix's powerful guitar, supported by Redding's bass and later by snare smacks and a punching kick drum from Mitchell. The song was inducted into the Grammy Hall of Fame in 2000 and it remains a staple on classic rock stations.

JIMI HENDRIX STATUE

1604 BROADWAY, SEATTLE

How do you immortalize someone who was born locally but affected the world? One who arguably has had the largest impact on guitar but who came up carrying his own gear like anyone else? Well, you do it in bronze, of course! Such is the case with the Jimi Hendrix statue, officially known as "the Electric Lady Studio Guitar," located in the Capitol Hill neighborhood at the corner of Broadway and East Pine. The near-life-sized homage to the late guitarist, which was created by sculptor Daryl Smith, was unveiled to the public in 1997.

The statue displays Hendrix shredding on his knees with his signature Stratocaster, playing as much for the gods as for the earthbound audience. The inspiration for the pose comes from Hendrix's performance at the 1967 Monterey International Pop Festival—the same show where he famously set his guitar on fire during the song "Wild Thing."

At the Hendrix statue, visitors leave flowers, notes, or take selfies. Some even leave the occasional "jazz cigarette." In 2013, the statue was vandalized by two men who purchased spray paint in the adjacent art store and defaced Hendrix. They were later arrested after being caught with literal paint on their hands. Since then, the statue has seen other acts of besmirchment, but thankfully nothing permanent.

The statue was originally conceived as part of a series of statues in Capitol Hill, commissioned by businessman and music lover Michael Malone. Others included Elvis Presley, Chuck Berry, and Buddy Holly. But today only Smith's Hendrix statue remains, displaying his '60s attire, expressive face, individual guitar strings, and textured hair.

Hendrix, who wrote hits like "Purple Haze" and "Foxy Lady," became famous from humble Emerald City beginnings. He grew up in the 1950s in the Central District, just a few minutes from the statue's location. Today, there are several more shrines to the artist throughout the city, but it's the statue that captures him best, frozen in musical ecstasy.

MERRILEE RUSH

SINGLE: "ANGEL OF THE MORNING"

RECORD: ANGEL OF THE MORNING

RELEASED: 1968 | **RECORDED IN:** SEATTLE

PRODUCER: TOMMY COGBILL, CHIPS MOMAN | **LABEL:** BELL RECORDS

Written in 1967 by songwriter Chip Taylor—who wrote the track after listening to the Rolling Stones song "Ruby Tuesday," penning it first for artist Connie Francis (who turned it down) and then for Evie Sands—"Angel of the Morning" was made famous by Seattle-born singer Merrilee Rush in 1968. (Taylor also wrote the iconic hit "Wild Thing.")

Born Merrilee Gunst on January 26, 1944, Rush earned fame in the Pacific Northwest performing at teenage dance clubs, a contemporary with PNW groups like the Fabulous Wailers. Later, she found herself in Memphis on tour with the Northwest standouts, Paul Revere & the Raiders. There, she recorded a solo demo of "Angel of the Morning" and knocked it out of the park. Upon its release, the single changed her career and introduced her to folks like Dick Clark of *American Bandstand*. "Angel of the Morning," which was ahead of its time, hinged on the idea of female and sexual empowerment, and Rush's sweet but sultry voice was a perfect fit. The track peaked

at No. 7 on the Billboard Hot 100 in 1968 and garnered the singer a Grammy nomination for Best Contemporary-Pop Vocal Performance, Female. Since then, it's been covered by many artists, including Juice Newton in 1981 and the rapper Shaggy in 2001. Rush released her own self-titled album in 1977.

The 1970s

NANCY WILSON ON THE SEATTLE SOUND AND THE FOUNDATIONAL 1970s

For Nancy Wilson, the guitar dynamo for the Pacific Northwest—born rock band Heart, Seattle has often reminded her of another cloudy port town that helped spawn a musical movement. Wilson, who rose to fame co-writing and performing songs like "Barracuda" and "Crazy On You," believes Seattle is a lot like the birthplace of the Beatles, Liverpool. But Seattle, notes Wilson, also has its own Fab Four: grunge icons Nirvana, Pearl Jam, Alice in Chains, and Soundgarden. Coincidence? Likely not.

"I always called Seattle the Liverpool of the States," says Wilson. "They are sister cities. Seattle is such a rich and storied seaport town with ferries crossing the Sound under gray rainy skies."

Heart, in which Wilson starred along with her big-voiced sister, lead singer Ann, released its seminal debut album, *Dreamboat Annie*, in 1975. With it, the band helped bolster the 1970s rock landscape, along with groups like Led Zeppelin and the Who. Of course, Heart was also different from these groups. They were American and were led by women. In this way, Heart inspired a generation (and

beyond) of rockers, from Kathleen Hanna to Brandi Carlile.

But, says Wilson, while rock thrived in the 1970s and later in the 1990s, the genre may have been searching for itself a bit in the 1980s. Indeed, she says, the '70s and the '90s were high points in the guitar-based music—thanks in large part to Seattle.

"The musical story of Seattle was never more fashionable than in the '90s," says Wilson. "The music was a much-needed break from the corporate '80s sound and literally put electric guitar rock back on the map. Nirvana, Alice in Chains, Pearl Jam, and Soundgarden became the pillars of the new sound that took over the world like a cultural flash mob."

While Wilson celebrates the grunge movement of the '90s, she knows it would not have happened without those who came before, including her skeleton-shaking rock group and the many others who preceded her, locally and beyond.

"Jimi Hendrix hailed from Seattle as well as great Northwest rock pioneers like the Wailers, Merrilee Rush and the Turnabouts, the Kingsmen, the Sonics, to name a few," says Wilson. "And then there was Ray Charles."

In Seattle, the question often arises, as it must also in pubs and music clubs in Liverpool today: Why here? What makes this place special and conducive to so much music? For Wilson, who has lived in the city for decades, including with her former husband of nearly twenty-five years, movie director Cameron Crowe, it has to do with location and weather as much as talent and drive.

"I think the moody weather of the great Northwest—like Liverpool—plus the infusion of sailors and travelers from around the world help bring forth a creative haven for players sheltering indoors out of the elements and banging away in garage bands," offers Wilson. "To me, all of these players through the eras are what makes 'The Seattle Sound.' The 50s bands informed the bands of the '60s and so forth."

Specifically, Wilson says, the '70s were a time of experimentation and achievement on the West Coast, thanks to open-minded cities like those in the Bay Area, as well as the Emerald City, and to musicians from Hendrix and Santana at Woodstock in 1969 to Heart and the second wave of the British invasion a handful of years later.

"In the '70s, Heart became part of the Seattle Sound although so much was also still being born

out of the Bay Area, too," Wilson says. "The mind-expanded sounds of the '60s folded easily into the '70s where you'd hear more epic and longer songs like 'In-A-Gadda-Da-Vida.' Also, the genius of Led Zeppelin entered the story like the ultimate rock muses they were, and it was at a small venue called the Green Lake Aqua Theater where we witnessed their opening set for a youth festival. It was as mind-bending and life-altering as having seen the Beatles live at the Seattle Coliseum in 1966."

And what effect, exactly, did all of this have on her in real time? "Being in Heart in the mid-'70s was pure adrenaline and excitement," says Wilson. "We had the intuition that music was a wide-open playing field for a band as unique as we were and that it was going to work. Apparently, our instincts were right when the first Heart album went big region by region in 1975."

What about the region itself? "All around the whole Northwest [in the '70s], that was a magical time for the Seattle Sound, even if you were from Vancouver or Portland or Olympia. Bands were thriving and creating greatness in their own right and in their own style. Later, the '80s decade was almost like rock had to get over its corporate tantrum to return to the real deal."

▲ Attendees in front of the fountain at Seattle Center during Bumbershoot music festival, Seattle, 1974

THE BLACK AND WHITE AFFAIR

SINGLE: "BOLD SOUL SISTER, BOLD SOUL BROTHER"

RECORD: BOLD SOUL SISTER, BOLD SOUL BROTHER

RELEASED: 1970 | **RECORDED IN:** SEATTLE

PRODUCER: KEARNEY BARTON | **LABEL:** TOPAZ RECORDS

This group started as the rhythm section for Mr. Clean and the Cleansers, which itself disbanded in 1967. From those ashes, though, emerged the Black and White Affair. Guitarist George Horton conceived of the name when the band was rushing to secure an overseas tour. Moniker in tow, the musicians first began recording with music pioneer Kearny Barton, who had already worked with notable acts like Quincy Jones and the Kingsmen.

Barton tracked the band's first singles, "Sweet Soul Lady" and "Until the Real Thing Comes Along," in Seattle for the record label Topaz. Those songs got airplay on local R & B radio. The band relocated to Los Angeles but never quite achieved the success it hoped there, due in large part to internal conflicts. So, they returned home to Seattle and continued to play.

Over the years, the group's lineup changed. Significant former members include Horton on guitar, Greg Barnes and Manuel Stanton on bass, multi-instrumentalist Lester MacFarland, and drummers James Adams, Wayne Bibb, Robbie Hill, and Dave Domineck. The group's song "Bold Soul Sister, Bold Soul Brother" opens with a fast-smacking snare, followed by looming organ chords and Calvin Law's soulful vocals. It's a timeless tune and a glimpse of the energy that the Black and White Affair brought to their shows.

A NOTE ON
WHEEDLE'S GROOVE

When one thinks about the Seattle sound, prominent grunge bands come to mind. Others, too, pop up like the punk bands from the riot grrrl movement. But there is another important era of music that is often overlooked when it comes to any Emerald City conversation, and that's the funk and soul movement of the '60s and '70s known now as "Wheedle's Groove." The music garnered attention in 2004 when the Seattle-born record label Light in the Attic released the record *Wheedle's Groove: Seattle's Finest in Funk & Soul 1965–75*. And a documentary followed in 2009, which includes narration by Sir Mix-a-Lot.

Light in the Attic label chiefs Matt Sullivan and Josh Wright took the funk and soul 45s they had collected from the region, including the 1974 cut "Wheedle's Groove" from the

Seattle-via-Spokane group Annakonda, and put them together in an 18-track compilation, re-releasing seminal songs from the era. To celebrate the collection, organizers put on a show at Seattle venue Chop Suey, where members of these funk and soul groups, then in their fifties and sixties, performed together as the "Wheedle's Groove" band. (The name "Wheedle" originates from a children's book about a fictional Pacific Northwest creature. Thanks to that book and the song, the Wheedle became the official mascot for the Space Needle and the Seattle SuperSonics.)

Wanting to keep the momentum going, Light in the Attic and the artists put on more shows, rotating members throughout the following years. Players included jazz pianist Overton Berry, organist Ron Buford, gospel powerhouse Pastor Pat Wright, Robbie Hill (drummer for the Black and White Affair), and percussionist Tony Gable of Cold, Bold & Together. This collection of musicians then worked with legendary producer Kearney Barton, who worked with early '50s and '60s garage rock bands like the Sonics, the Kingsmen, the Fabulous Wailers, and more, even collaborating with local big names like Quincy Jones and Nancy Wilson. Later, in 2009, *Kearney Barton* by Wheedle's Groove dropped, featuring new songs.

When remembering the funk and soul bands from the '60s and '70s in Seattle, groups to keep in mind include the Black and White Affair, Robbie Hill's Family Affair, Overton Berry, the Johnny Lewis Quartet, Cookin' Bag, Patrinell Staten (a.k.a. Pastor Pat Wright), and Cold, Bold & Together (which once featured Kenny G). Indeed, the musicians of Seattle's mid-twentieth-century funk and soul scene are as impactful in the region as any other, part of a movement that could have been lost to history. The Seattle weather didn't only inspire long-haired musicians wearing flannel, but was made more bearable with funky guitars, loud horns, and moaning organs.

GREGG ROLIE (SANTANA)

SINGLE: "OYE COMO VA"

RECORD: ABRAXAS

RELEASED: 1970 | **RECORDED IN:** SAN FRANCISCO

PRODUCER: FRED CATERO, CARLOS SANTANA | **LABEL:** COLUMBIA RECORDS

Born in Seattle in 1947, Gregg Rolie became one of the most significant voices in '60s and '70s rock music, a cofounder and lead vocalist of bands like Santana and Journey. The two-time Rock & Roll Hall of Fame inductee left the Emerald City for the Bay Area in 1965, a year after high school, where with Carlos Santana he formed the guitarist's eponymous group. With Santana, Rolie performed at the original Woodstock, helping to grow the legend of the psychedelic rock group. He sang on Santana's early hits, including "Oye Como Va," from the album *Abraxas*. He also sang on the track "Black Magic Woman."

In 1972, Santana completed the album *Caravanserai*, but that's when Rolie and guitarist Neal Schon decided to leave the outfit and start a new one. Rolie went back home to Seattle to regroup and soon after, he and Schon formed Journey. Rolie sang lead vocals on several albums, eventually sharing duties with Steve Perry. In 1980, he left the band and began to release solo records featuring Schon, Santana, and other pals. In 2012, Rolie toured as a member of Ringo Starr's "All Starr Band," singing hits from the Santana catalog. Rolie's voice matched the material—with a smooth timbre and a hint of friction.

Today, the vocalist lives outside another musical metropolis, Austin, Texas, where he no doubt is lending his voice and experience to more songs. But what he achieved in the mid-twentieth century with two iconic and internationally known bands will forever live on in history.

SEATTLE
CENTER

305 HARRISON STREET, SEATTLE

Developed for the 1962 World's Fair, which brought the Space Needle and Elvis (and his film crew) to the Emerald City, Seattle Center remains a hub for music and other important events. At the intersection of Belltown and Queen Anne, the area spans nearly seventy-five acres and is home to Bumbershoot and Northwest Folklife festivals. Both founded in 1971, they continue to bookend the summer. At each, fans can see established international acts as well as up-and-coming local ones from the city's own backyard (not to mention diverse food, crafts, and more).

Seattle Center is also where KEXP is located. From the shadow of the Space Needle, once the tallest structure west of the Mississippi, the popular independent radio station broadcasts its diverse sounds to an ardent global audience. It's also where international bands like the Smile and Big Joanie, and locals like La Fonda, come to record in-studio performances.

Adjacent to the KEXP building is Climate Pledge Arena. Formerly Key Arena, the massive venue on any night could be showcasing acts like Coldplay, Billie Eilish, Foo Fighters, Dave Matthews, or ODESZA to sold-out audiences. On non-musical nights, the space is home to the WNBA champion Seattle Storm and the NHL hockey team the Seattle Kraken; and, many hope, it will one day be home again to the Seattle SuperSonics NBA team.

For those who want more than just music, Seattle Center is also home to Chihuly Garden and Glass, displaying artist Dale Chihuly's iconic blown glass work; the Pacific Science Center; the Museum of Pop Culture (formerly the EMP); and the Seattle Children's Museum.

And while the 1963 Elvis film *It Happened at the World's Fair* was a flop, it still managed to showcase Seattle's growth and looming potential. The city was no longer a logging outpost. It was now a hub of technology and entertainment. For Presley's character and the ten million visitors to the World's Fair that year, Seattle marked a new era. Today, Seattle Center serves as a reminder of where the region has been and what might be next.

CAROL KAYE

SINGLE: "AMERICA THE BEAUTIFUL"

RECORD: A MESSAGE FROM THE PEOPLE

RELEASED: 1972 | **RECORDED IN:** LOS ANGELES

PRODUCER: QUINCY JONES | **LABEL:** ABC

Everett, Washington's Carol Kaye, who was the daughter of professional musicians, was around music from the moment she could hear. Today, she is an example of someone who had a rich career but who was also in the background. Early in her career, Kaye began working with Brian Wilson of the Beach Boys, appearing on songs like "Good Vibrations," and with controversial producer Phil Spector. Then . . . local legend Quincy Jones.

Kaye's session work ultimately led to her role in the iconic Los Angeles-based session band the Wrecking Crew, which played on recordings of countless hits for popular bands. It was a group Dick Clark said "had the magic touch." Kaye, who received her first guitar in 1948 at thirteen, was a savant. She learned quickly and was playing professionally just a year later. First it was clubs, arranged by her own guitar teacher, Horace Hatchett. But in 1957,

she was asked to work on a recording
of "Summertime" by Sam Cooke, and she
knew that there could be a more stable,
fruitful life in music outside clubs
and bars.

While Kaye, known for her sunglasses and
melodic bass lines, started her career
playing the six-string guitar, she
moved onto bass in 1963. Why? Another
bass player had failed to show up for a
session, so she filled in and, in that
moment, found her calling.

During her prolific career, Kaye played
on songs performed by Frank Sinatra,
Sonny & Cher, the Beach Boys, Quincy
Jones, Herb Alpert, Bobby Womack, Ray
Charles, Burt Bacharach, Nancy Sinatra,
Neil Young, and more. She's the bass
player on the *Mission Impossible*
theme. She performed sound effects on
Steven Spielberg's first television
movie, *Duel*. And she played on Ray
Charles's 1972 version of "America the
Beautiful," a song considered one of
the world's most beautiful and patri-
otic, and recorded by an artist once
based in Seattle. Although session
musicians often aren't household names,
she was one of, if not *the*, best in the
business. In fact, Wilson later called
her the "greatest damn bass player in
the world."

HEART

SINGLE: "CRAZY ON YOU"

RECORD: DREAMBOAT ANNIE

RELEASED: 1975 | **RECORDED IN:** VANCOUVER, BC

PRODUCER: MIKE FLICKER | **LABEL:** MUSHROOM

The rock band Heart formed officially in 1973. The group, which included powerhouse vocalist Ann Wilson, guitarist Roger Fisher, bassist Steve Fossen, drummer Michael Derosier, and multi-instrumentalist Howard Leese, then recruited Ann's six-string-playing younger sister, Nancy. With her addition, Heart was complete.

In 1975, the band released its debut LP, *Dreamboat Annie*, which peaked at No. 7 on the Billboard 200 and included hits like "Magic Man" and "Crazy on You." On "Crazy on You," the opening song from the debut LP, an acoustic riff from Nancy begins before Ann offers her stirring voice. The song was inspired by turbulent times in the world, like the Vietnam War. Nancy says the track was like a "call to your partner," the sonic equivalent of "I know the world is just insanely crazy here right now. But I just want us to go crazy together. To let it all just fall away so it's only just you and me here."

Decades after its release, the chorus from
the song was sampled by rap star Eminem.
He even brought the sisters together for a
"top-secret" meeting to talk about its production. The resulting track, "Crazy in
Love," is yet another example of the power of
the sisters. Ann and Nancy, who released sixteen albums as Heart, also undertook a less-
er-known acoustic side project, Lovemongers,
which included a covers EP in 1992 and a studio LP in 1997.

KEXP

472 1ST AVENUE N, SEATTLE

How do you become one of the most celebrated public radio stations in the world? For the Seattle indie music station, KEXP, with its studio located in the shadow of the Space Needle, the answer begins on the campus of the University of Washington. Started in 1972, the outfit was known in its nascent days as KCMU. Founded by four undergraduates and originally located in the university's communications building, the station later changed its call sign and broadcast from Dexter Avenue before moving to Seattle Center.

The name comes from the late billionaire Paul Allen. The Microsoft cofounder started his Experience Music Project—now the Museum of Pop Culture—in Seattle Center, and so the city's indie rock station adapted its call letters to reflect that. KEXP is now the most popular non-NPR public radio station in the United States thanks to its DJs and the freedom it gives them to play whatever music they choose. It has championed many unknown artists and helped launch the careers of others like Macklemore & Ryan Lewis.

The list of DJs, both past and present, employed at the station is extensive. It includes an author of this book (Eva Walker), a Sub Pop Records cofounder (Jonathan Poneman), and a radio icon (Marco Collins). Its current stable includes Cheryl Waters, John Richards, Kevin Cole, Larry Mizel Jr., and more. Outside of its airplay, the station is well-known around the globe for its in-studio performances, which have featured musicians like Florence and the Machine, Wet Leg, the Smile, Lizzo, and others.

KEXP, which expanded its broadcast to San Francisco in 2023, is also known for its remote broadcasts in France, Iceland, Mexico, and Argentina. Its facility in Seattle Center includes a café, record shop, and public gathering space. In 2020, the station grew significantly after witnessing the global protests in the wake of George Floyd's murder. There has since been a dedicated effort toward equitable and antiracist work.

As the station forges on, it's become a place for so many to find and discover music, from tourists to hopeful musicians, local music lovers, and global fans. Machines don't program playlists at KEXP; rather, content is curated by the keen folks behind the mics. Their ears are helping to shape the sonic landscape twenty-four hours a day, seven days a week, in Seattle and beyond.

The
1980s

"THE GRUNGEFATHER" JACK ENDINO ON SEATTLE'S GROWING INDIE SCENE

Thank goodness for moms. If it weren't for Jack Endino's mother, who was originally from the Northwest, the world may be a very different place. Endino moved to the Seattle area from Connecticut in 1974 with his parents, who regularly listened to Herb Alpert, Frank Sinatra, and Duke Ellington records. But it was in the early '70s that the young Endino noticed popular radio. Even today, his favorite thing about producing songs is the "hooks," those bits of music that stick in your head and won't let go. "That's what it's all about," he says.

Growing up in the area in the '70s, bands like Heart and BTO were on the air. Endino, who would grow up to help define a musical era, says he had a sense of regional music at the time. He noticed that some bands being played on the radio in Seattle didn't make it to the East Coast airwaves and vice versa. For instance, the Australian rockers AC/DC were popular in Seattle before they hit it big in the rest of the country, the city being one of the first markets to play the band.

But it wasn't until Endino, who turned twenty-one in 1979, went to college at the University of Washington that things began to fall into place.

All along what's known as "the Ave," or University Way NE, the main thoroughfare around UW, Endino saw record stores. At any given time, there would be three or four used shops along a five- or six-block stretch. He'd "bounce around" from one to the other, thumbing through the stacks. He'd gotten into mainstream radio while living in the region with his family. But he didn't have access to records until he came to the Ave.

"Pretty much the entire history of rock music was sitting in these used bins," says Endino. "I went nuts—I lost my mind!"

At the time, record stores were perhaps the central portal to a wealth of music. In addition, there were *Rolling Stone* and *Creem* magazines. But there was no internet, no social media. So, people bought and traded records. Endino "went deep." It was this less formal education that helped him internalize a range of sounds. All of a sudden, he was becoming an encyclopedia. And it's with this foundation that Endino's legendary career began.

After college, Endino moved to Bremerton to work in the naval shipyard. There, he played some, jamming with the fellas. He wasn't connected to the Seattle scene. But he did buy a four-track recorder to teach himself how to work it. When he moved back to Seattle in 1984, he moved into a friend's basement, set up his four-track, and shortly thereafter started his influential rock band, Skin Yard. The first drummer? Matt Cameron (who later went on to Soundgarden and Pearl Jam).

Skin Yard opened up a world of connections, friends, and collaborations. At the same time, an indie network was starting to form between clubs, zines, and the like. This provided a rudimentary infrastructure that spanned the whole United States, a circuit that allowed bands to tour and maybe even break even. At the same time, indie labels began to pop up, Endino says—from San Francisco, Los Angeles, DC, New York, Chicago, and other cities. So, Sub Pop founders (and Endino's friends) Bruce Pavitt and Jonathan Poneman thought, why not Seattle? And Sub Pop Records was born.

Endino began recording bands in his little basement studio in 1985 and started working at Reciprocal Recording in 1986. His first clients were Green River and Soundgarden—before even Sub Pop got involved. The now iconic *Deep Six* album was released that same year through C/Z Records. The brainchild of Chris Hanzsek, who owned Reciprocal, the compilation included Skin Yard, Melvins, Malfunkshun, Soundgarden, Green River, and the U-Men. With that, a movement began. The album showcased a new sound and, coupled with the recordings Endino did at Reciprocal with Green River and Soundgarden, Sub Pop had material.

"The *Deep Six* record was a totally different kettle of fish," Endino says.

Endino began to work fast and prolifically with the burgeoning Sub Pop. He estimates he recorded 42 to 50 of the first 100 Sub Pop releases, many of which were 7-inch vinyl. Today, Endino acts like Seattle's very own Library of Congress, at least when it comes to rock and grunge history. He's even diving back into some of the records he recorded with bands like Green River and the Fluid, now that he has more time, perspective, and experience. He's like a movie director, creating a new cut. He's revisiting bands like Bam Bam, IMIJ, Mudhoney, and Soundgarden. Even some obscure

Nirvana recordings are getting fresh listens.

"With *Bleach*," says Endino of Nirvana's debut, which he recorded in thirty hours for $606.17, "We were feeling pretty good that day. I got good tones, the band was good. It was done pretty painlessly. But not everything that was made during that classic grunge era was all that hi-fi."

When you're the Grungefather, as Endino is affectionately called, you get to dive back in and take another pass for reissues and re-releases. Truly, Endino's career took shape in the eye of the grunge storm. His ex-wife, Dawn Anderson, wrote the review of the *Deep Six* album in Seattle's iconic and now-defunct music publication, *The Rocket*. Endino knows the history of heavy stuff in Seattle from the late '70s and into the '80s too. Bands like Metal Church, which, while not connected directly to the grunge scene, did impact it in tangential ways. When Anderson wrote about *Deep Six*, she knew what was happening.

"She basically says in the article, 'We need a new name for this,'" says Endino. "She didn't have the name. But she knew it wasn't metal, wasn't punk. It was this new oozing mess of music. A regional sound that was coalescing. So, what are we going to call it?"

The term *grunge* came a few years after *Deep Six*, though, to this day, no one knows from where exactly. Like Anderson, Endino could feel the difference in this sound. He could see the artists sharing influences, from heavier stuff to British post-punk to '70s riff rock. By 1986 or 1987, he could feel the wave rising. Zines were important, as was *The Rocket* and its editor Charles R. Cross, who would later write seminal biographies about Kurt Cobain and Jimi Hendrix.

Endino says it was around 1991 when he saw the wave, not crashing, but getting too large. Surely, a devastating fall would come. Record companies were everywhere. In the span of months, Alice in Chains, Soundgarden, Screaming Trees, Nirvana, and Pearl Jam all released albums. Sir Mix-a-Lot was about to earn a Grammy and garner a No. 1 song with his ode to posteriors. The world had officially changed, with Seattle playing a key role. But if it wasn't for Endino's mother, who decided to come back to her Northwest roots, none of this may have transpired (or at least sounded as good).

"It's lovely," says Endino of his place in history. "I found myself plunged into the whole indie music scene thing—it snowballed from there."

QUINCY JONES

SINGLE: "ONE HUNDRED WAYS"

RECORD: THE DUDE

RELEASED: 1981 | **RECORDED IN:** LOS ANGELES

PRODUCER: QUINCY JONES | **LABEL:** A&M RECORDS

Born in Chicago in 1933, Quincy Jones moved to Bremerton during World War II with his parents and siblings. There, his father got a job working at the Puget Sound Naval Shipyard. After the war, they moved to Seattle proper, where Jones attended—and developed his skills on trumpet at—Garfield High School. At fourteen, Quincy, nicknamed "Quick" for his speed on trumpet, first met a sixteen-year-old Ray Charles when he performed at the city's Black Elks Club.

Jones later attended Seattle University and, while attending what is now the Berklee College of Music, began touring with pianist Lionel Hampton, eventually moving to New York City where he worked as an arranger for artists like Count Basie, Sarah Vaughn, and Duke Ellington, as well as his close friend by then, Ray Charles. Since then, Jones has produced many hits with artists

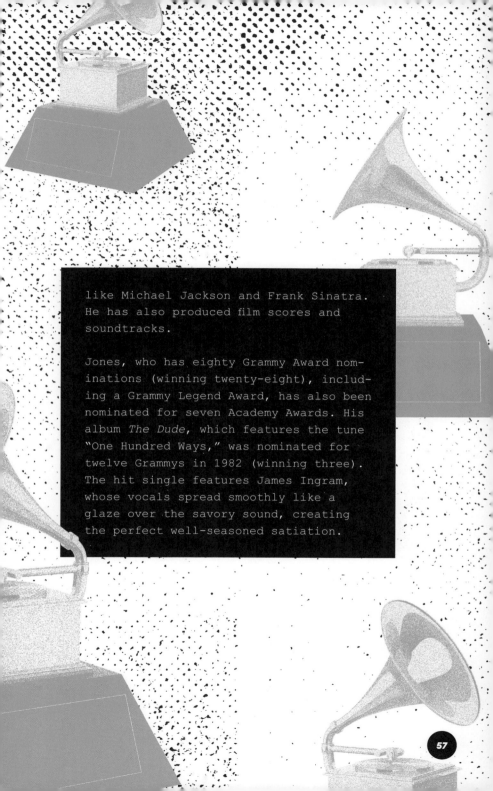

like Michael Jackson and Frank Sinatra.
He has also produced film scores and
soundtracks.

Jones, who has eighty Grammy Award nominations (winning twenty-eight), including a Grammy Legend Award, has also been
nominated for seven Academy Awards. His
album *The Dude*, which features the tune
"One Hundred Ways," was nominated for
twelve Grammys in 1982 (winning three).
The hit single features James Ingram,
whose vocals spread smoothly like a
glaze over the savory sound, creating
the perfect well-seasoned satiation.

A NOTE ON
GARFIELD
HIGH SCHOOL

"Garfield High School for me was an epicenter of the classic age, the golden era, the *vendange* of this city. So many people in the Seattle community had and have walked those halls, spent their formative years dipped into the culture and came out uniquely spiced, heading out into the world as young adults. GHS was and is a place full of legends. As a child, I heard stories of genius musicians, spectacular sports stars, innovative burglars, movie stars, street fighters, champions, dope dealers, mean coaches, pretty ladies, tough dudes, crazy teachers, and artists of all ilk swirling in an atmosphere rich with excitement, danger, and pride. When you left there, you had more than anything acquired a proprietary intelligence that made you feel confident in any future place you may find yourself. And when I got there, it surpassed even that magnificent anticipation."

—*Ishmael Butler, class of '87*
frontman for the Grammy-winning Digable Planets

THE FARTZ

SINGLE: "IDIOTS RULE"

RECORD: BECAUSE THIS FUCKIN' WORLD STINKS . . .

RELEASED: 1981 | **RECORDED IN:** SEATTLE

PRODUCER: NEIL HUBBARD, THE FARTZ | **LABEL:** FARTZ RECORDS

Founded in 1981, the Fartz were a pioneering hardcore punk band from Seattle, often railing against political and social injustices with fast-paced, aggressive music. Fronted by Blaine Cook, an actual chef who later ran his own burger restaurant, the group's original lineup included guitar player Tommy Hansen, bassist Steve Hofmann, and drummer Loud Fart. Like the New York City band the Ramones, everyone in the Fartz took the last name "Fart." Thanks to the debut EP, *Because This Fuckin' World Stinks . . .*, the members signed to the San Francisco label Alternative Tentacles.

In 1982, the band released its debut LP, *World Full of Hate*. In the summer of that year, Loud Fart was replaced on the drum kit by none other than Duff McKagan, future bassist for Guns N' Roses. In the end, Duff wasn't with the group for very long, and in truth, the Fartz themselves weren't around for that long, only sticking together from 1981 to 1983. In that time, the band became known as part of a seminal West Coast hardcore punk triad, which also included the

Dead Kennedys from the Bay Area and D.O.A. from Vancouver, BC.

After the Fartz disbanded, several of the members founded the important Seattle-based group, 10 Minute Warning, which also included McKagan and was a precursor for popular grunge bands to follow. In 1984, Cook also took on the role as lead singer for the seminal thrash outfit The Accüsed. In the late '90s, renewed interest in the Fartz and their catalog propelled the group to release new work in the early 2000s. But it's their early aggressive rock, showcased in abundance on the 1981 track "Idiots Rule," that made them required listening a decade before bands like Nirvana and Pearl Jam would rule the airwaves.

THE EMERALD STREET BOYS

SINGLE: "CHRISTMAS RAP"

RECORD: CHRISTMAS RAP

RELEASED: 1983 | **RECORDED IN:** SEATTLE

PRODUCER: TONY BENTON | **LABEL:** TELEMUSIC PRODUCTIONS

We can't talk about the history of Seattle music without recognizing the city's first-ever rap group, the Emerald Street Boys. The group, which has influenced and inspired local Grammy Award-winning artists like Sir Mix-a-Lot and Ishmael Butler of Digable Planets, was composed of RC Jamerson, Ed "Sugarbear" Wells, and James "Captain Crunch" Croone.

Jamerson, who attended Nathan Hale High School in North Seattle, heard his first hip-hop song in 1979. That track? "Rapper's Delight" by New York City collective the Sugarhill Gang. Hearing this, Jamerson's future became clear to him, and it definitely included rap. When he connected with Wells and Croone, the trio came up with their group's moniker and recorded what is now recognized as Seattle's first hip-hop song.

"Christmas Rap" is a fun and funky holiday jam that represents the feelings and joy of the holiday season circa 1983. Playfully providing their own twist on "Rudolph the Red-Nosed Reindeer" about halfway through the song, it's clear why the Emerald Street Boys will "go down in history," as the traditional "Rudolph" song says. Without their early contribution and influence on the city's history, along with those of other early local rap pioneers like Jam Delight, Silver Chain Gang, and DJ "Nasty" Nes, there might be no Mix, Ish, or Macklemore!

TINA BELL (BAM BAM)

SINGLE: "VILLAINS (ALSO WEAR WHITE)"

RECORD: VILLAINS (ALSO WEAR WHITE)

RELEASED: 1984 | **RECORDED IN:** SEATTLE

PRODUCER: CHRIS HANZSEK, TOMMY MARTIN | **LABEL:** SELF-RELEASED

Did you know grunge has a godmother? Born in Seattle on February 5, 1957, Tina Bell began singing at Mount Zion Baptist Church on 19th Avenue. She later hit the stage for the first time at the Langston Hughes Performing Arts Institute in the Central District. While working on a play for the theater, Bell met future husband and bandmate Tommy Martin. Their relationship would go on to impact local music forever.

In 1983, Bell and Martin formed Bam Bam (an abbreviation of "Bell And Martin"). The original lineup also included Scott "Buttocks" Ledgerwood and Matt Cameron, who later joined Soundgarden and Pearl Jam. Tom Hendrickson joined the band after Cameron's departure. At only five-foot-two, Bell's size didn't keep her from often being the biggest person in the room. Whatever the venue, her powerful vocals and punk attitude ruled. She retained control, even when dealing with racial attacks.

Villains (Also Wear White) is about just that. Many communities have been taught to villainize darkness, consciously or unconsciously. Dark clothing usually implies evil and white clothing is regularly seen as angelic or superior. This has been applied to skin color as well. *Villains (Also Wear White)* disputes this. The album was recorded at Reciprocal Recording, where Nirvana would later track their demos for *Bleach*. Studio owner Chris Hanzsek has said Bam Bam was the first band he recorded on vinyl.

Bam Bam went on to perform at numerous spots around town, sharing bills with groups like Alice in Chains, Pearl Jam, and Soundgarden in the '80s. Bell eventually left the band in 1990 and ultimately music altogether. She passed away in October of 2012 at the age of fifty-five in Las Vegas but has recently been rediscovered and celebrated for her contributions to grunge.

CENTRAL
SALOON

207 1ST AVENUE S. SEATTLE

There is a hidden city underneath Seattle. At least, the remains of it. When the Great Seattle Fire struck in 1889 and blocks of Pioneer Square were leveled, those rebuilding the area decided to just build on top of the rubble. In the heart of that rebuild some hundred-plus years later stands the iconic Central Saloon, home to many underground acts that later became top shelf.

Inside, you can see large murals of rapper Sir Mix-a-Lot and rocker Tina Bell. On the opposite wall, there are a slew of show posters lined up from the '90s displaying band names like Screaming Trees, Nirvana, Soundgarden, Love Battery, Skin Yard, Alice in Chains, and more.

Established in 1892, the venue was also the site of Nirvana's first-ever show in Seattle, helping Kurt Cobain and the Aberdeen-born band to sign to Sub Pop, a mere ninety-nine years after the Great Fire.

The place is so beloved that in the summer of 2022, the owners of the venue bought the building, making sure the landmark wouldn't get razed for another high-rise of condos. Today, the venue is known as the birthplace of grunge. Throughout the space's hundred-plus-year history, it has also been a post office and a brothel. A hub first bolstered by the Yukon Gold Rush, the venue has more recently opened the door for gold records.

THE U-MEN

SINGLE: "GILA"

RECORD: U-MEN

RELEASED: 1984 | **RECORDED IN:** SEATTLE

PRODUCER: JOHN NELSON | **LABEL:** BOMB SHELTER

Formed in Seattle in 1980, the U-Men had a major influence on grunge, despite breaking onto the scene about a decade prior. In 1983, the band became the first group to be managed by Susan Silver, the now-renowned former manager for other groups like Alice in Chains and Soundgarden.

At their height, the U-Men were known as one of the most entertaining local live acts during an era where stage prowess was especially prized. Others rivaling the U-Men's enthusiasm include Rail (who toured with Van Halen and Heart), the Heats, the Puds, X-15, Student Nurse, the Macs, and the Blackouts. Many of these were featured on the seminal rock compilation *Seattle Syndrome*, released in 1981 on Engram Records.

The U-Men were so influential that the Butthole Surfers named their song "The

O-Men" in honor of the outfit. While the U-Men disbanded in 1989 before grunge took hold, their entire catalog was remastered by "Grungefather" Jack Endino and re-released on Sub Pop Records in 2017. Their song "Gila," which was originally released as a split single with Melvins, clocks in at just over two minutes. It's a guitar- and bass-driven banger held together by propulsive drums as frontman John Bigley's vocals batter the beat.

ROBERT CRAY

SINGLE: "SMOKING GUN"

RECORD: STRONG PERSUADER

RELEASED: 1986 | **RECORDED IN:** LOS ANGELES

PRODUCER: BRUCE BROMBERG, DENNIS WALKER | **LABEL:** MERCURY RECORDS

Born in Georgia in 1953, Robert Cray later relocated to Tacoma with his family, and he attended Lakes High School in Lakewood, Washington. There, he found friends who all seemed to have their own guitars and garages for rocking out. Yet it wasn't until a few years later that Cray and his guitar-playing pals would become interested in playing the blues.

Listening to musicians like B. B. King, Howlin' Wolf, and Buddy Guy, Cray and his friends dreamed of becoming blues stars themselves. Releasing twenty-one studio albums, winning five Grammy Awards and topping several music charts, Cray has since been inducted into the Blues Hall of Fame. He also received the Americana Music Lifetime Achievement Award for Performance in 2017 by the Americana Music Association.

His record *Strong Persuader*, which features the track "Smoking Gun," was certified two-times platinum, with "Smoking Gun" hitting No. 22 on the Billboard Hot 100. It also received an MTV Music

Video Award nomination for Best New Artist in
a Video for the song. "Smoking Gun" is a song
about infidelity and the singer's conflicted feelings about his love for someone else. It's the
combination of Cray's heartbroken vocals with
an equally forlorn guitar that makes this song
strike a chord many decades later.

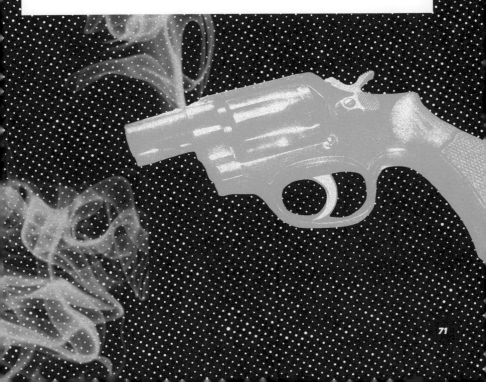

DEEMS

SINGLE: "TOUGH TOFU"

RECORD: LIVING

RELEASED: 1986 | **RECORDED IN:** SEATTLE

PRODUCER: DEEMS TSUTAKAWA, RICK FISHER

LABEL: J-TOWN RECORDS

The son of renowned painter and sculptor George Tsutakawa, Deems Tsutakawa was born and raised in Seattle and began playing piano at the age of five. But it wasn't until he was a teenager that his playing shifted from classical to other styles of more popular music—most prominently jazz.

Deems studied ethnomusicology, art, and drama at the University of Washington, deciding along his academic journey to attempt a full-fledged career in music. He founded J-Town Records in 1977, releasing his first 45 for the single "Okashi Na," which was followed by his debut self-titled LP in 1982. The song "Tough Tofu" is from his second studio album, *Living*, released in 1986. That song is a funky jazz tune, which is perhaps unexpected given its silly title.

The track opens with a single snare
hit, immediately followed by bass and
guitar. Deems arrives with a glissando
down the piano keys, jumping into a
memorable riff. The guitar and piano
complement one another throughout
the phrasing until they're united at
the end of each section with staccato
stylings, making this a song you just
have to move to and vibe with.

SKIN YARD

SINGLE: "REPTILE"

RECORD: SKIN YARD

RELEASED: 1987 | **RECORDED IN:** SEATTLE

PRODUCER: SKIN YARD | **LABEL:** C/Z RECORDS

Tucked away in a respected recording studio in Seattle's Ballard neighborhood, Jack Endino works daily, tracking up-and-coming and established bands. To most, he's like any other skilled engineer, turning knobs and making pointed suggestions. But the eagle-eyed will spot the Latin Grammy Award on the counter. If asked, he'll say his *Bleach* platinum plaque is in a box somewhere. Clearly, Endino is no ordinary musician—he's a legend.

He even has a nickname: the Grungefather. The man who played guitar and produced the music for the '80s popular rock group Skin Yard recorded some of the most iconic bands in the Emerald City, including Nirvana for their debut LP. He also recorded Soundgarden and Skin Yard's self-titled debut.

Comprised of Endino on guitar, Ben McMillan on vocals and sax, Daniel House on bass, and Jason Finn (of the Presidents of the United States of America) and Matt Cameron on drums, Skin Yard's debut LP was a local hit and

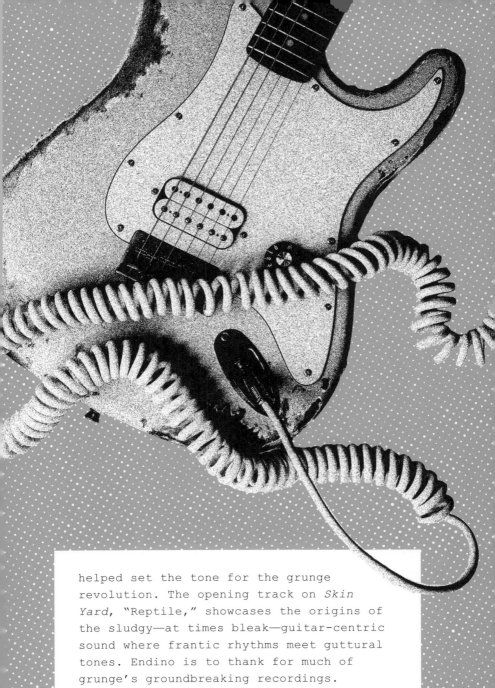

helped set the tone for the grunge
revolution. The opening track on *Skin
Yard*, "Reptile," showcases the origins of
the sludgy—at times bleak—guitar-centric
sound where frantic rhythms meet guttural
tones. Endino is to thank for much of
grunge's groundbreaking recordings.

EASY STREET RECORDS

4559 CALIFORNIA AVENUE SW, SEATTLE

Located in the heart of West Seattle, Easy Street Records is a local music beacon. It was founded in 1988 when Matt Vaughan, then a student at Seattle University working at two record stores both set to close, decided to consolidate the stores and run his own. Thirty years later, the place was voted by *Rolling Stone* and *Time* magazines as one of the ten best record stores in the United States. Since opening Easy Street, Vaughan has seen friends like members of Alice in Chains rise to stardom. Vaughan helped sell records by Sir Mix-a-Lot when the rapper began hustling his albums. Likewise, he was there to help a young Macklemore early on.

Home to countless vinyl albums, CDs, and tapes, along with other merchandise like T-shirts and movies, Easy Street is a community hub. It is also home to a quirky café, with music-themed offerings like the Woody Guthrie Farmers Omelet and the New Wave O's Rancheros, and a modest stage for bands that's been graced by everyone from the Sonics to Pearl Jam. But it wasn't always easy to keep the place going. The retail music market has experienced major fluctuations over the years (although these days vinyl records are breaking new sales marks).

Through hard work and a knack for knowing what's good, Vaughan has forged bonds with groups like the Head and the Heart and labels like Sub Pop. And whether it's Record Store Day or just a sunny Sunday morning, Easy Street is an ideal destination (along with other local shops like Sonic Boom in Ballard and Jive Time in Fremont) to spend a few minutes or several hours.

DIANE SCHUUR

SINGLE: "TRAV'LIN LIGHT"

RECORD: DIANE SCHUUR &
THE COUNT BASIE ORCHESTRA

RELEASED: 1987 | **RECORDED IN:** LOS ANGELES

PRODUCER: MORGAN AMES, JEFFREY WEBER | **LABEL:** GRP

Released in 1987, the live album *Diane Schuur & the Count Basie Orchestra* stayed atop the Billboard jazz charts for thirty-three weeks. It also earned a Grammy for Schuur for the category Best Jazz Vocal Performance, Female. Recorded some three years after legendary musician Count Basie died, his namesake orchestra was led by Frank Foster.

Born in Tacoma in 1953, Schuur arrived as a premature infant, weighing less than three pounds. This caused her to lose her vision. (She later received a financial settlement from her birth hospital as a result.) Due to his early birth, her twin brother also suffered from hearing loss. Nicknamed "Deedles," Schuur grew up in Auburn, Washington. As a kid, she enrolled in the Washington School for the Blind in Vancouver. Her parents (and the radio) introduced her to music early on, from Duke Ellington to Dinah Washington. And her attention

paid off. Later in life, Schuur would
become a two-time Grammy Award-winner.

Schuur's voice, which sounds like dusk
setting into evening, is rich and full,
lovely and lush. On her live rendition
of "Trav'lin Light," a song originally
made famous by Billie Holiday, Schuur
brings depth, vibrancy, and a reflective tone that soothes like a warm mug
of tea on a rainy Sunday. Schuur, with
twenty-six albums to date, released her
latest, *Running on Faith*, in 2020.

S·U·B
P·O·P

SUB POP
RECORDS
(ORIGINAL LOCATION)
**1932 1ST AVENUE, 11TH FLOOR,
SEATTLE**

"Only affordable because the elevator didn't go to the top floor."
—Sub Pop cofounder Bruce Pavitt

Established as a brick and mortar in 1988, Sub Pop Records has become one of the most prominent and respected independent record labels in the business. While everything began with Bruce Pavitt in the mid-1980s, the label really picked up steam in the latter half of the decade and into the '90s, thanks to the rise of grunge and Sub Pop bands like Nirvana, Mudhoney, and Soundgarden. Later, the label signed the Postal Service, Fleet Foxes, the Shins, Shabazz Palaces, and musical comedy duo Flight of the Conchords.

Initially, Sub Pop, first named *Subterranean Pop*, was a simple handmade fan zine started by Pavitt, an Evergreen State College student. The zine focused on independent labels around the country before eventually becoming one itself. A few years after starting his simple but passionate zine, Pavitt joined forces with KCMU (now KEXP) DJ Jonathan Poneman. Together,

their partnership would grow Sub Pop to great heights.

To date, Sub Pop posts two platinum-selling albums: the Postal Service's 2003 album *Give Up* and Nirvana's debut 1989 album *Bleach*. The label also enjoys seven gold-certified releases, including LPs from the Shins, Fleet Foxes, the Head and the Heart, and Band of Horses. Sub Pop also curates its regular Sub Pop Singles Club, which features vinyl pressings from various artists sent to subscribers. The very first was in 1988: Nirvana's "Love Buzz."

Today, the label's impressive roster includes bands like Beach House, the Head and the Heart, and Sleater-Kinney. Past single releases include L7, John Waters, the White Stripes, and Eddie Vedder. While the label's first location was downtown at 1932 1st Avenue in the Terminal Sales Building, the operation has grown and today, the label is headquartered at 2013 4th Avenue. If you happen to take a stroll near the old spot, take a moment to commune with the ghosts of grunge past.

BEAT HAPPENING

SINGLE: "INDIAN SUMMER"

RECORD: JAMBOREE

RELEASED: 1988 | **RECORDED IN:** ELLENSBURG, WA

PRODUCER: STEVE FISK, MARK LANEGAN, GARY LEE CONNER

LABEL: K RECORDS, ROUGH TRADE

The story of Beat Happening is the story of more than just the PNW rock group. It's also the story of frontman Calvin Johnson, an artist, curator, and founder of the prominent label K Records. Known for his deep, droning voice, Johnson also played roles in bands like Cool Rays and the Go Team. But his biggest achievement was founding K, which, along with Sub Pop, changed the face of local music distribution.

His band, Beat Happening, which formed in Olympia in 1982, was known for its prolific but often rudimentary recordings. There is a childlike quality about the group, including on their oft-covered song "Indian Summer." Johnson, often seen in ripped jeans and oversized sweatshirts, was a pioneer of local indie culture, helping to usher in groups like Bikini Kill and the riot grrrl movement.

Founded at Olympia's Evergreen State College, Beat Happening began to record in 1983. All the songs

from *Jamboree*, its seminal 1988 album, were produced by Steve Fisk, along with grunge icon Mark Lanegan and artist Gary Lee Conner. The album's songs "Bewitched" and "Indian Summer" were listed in a 2005 *Pitchfork* article on "twee pop" essential listening. And Dean Wareham, frontman for the New York indie band Luna, has called "Indian Summer" the equivalent of "indie's 'Knocking on Heaven's Door.'" Why? "Everybody's done it," he says.

The 1990s

SIR MIX-A-LOT ON
SEATTLE'S MUSICAL EXPLOSION

When Grammy Award–winning rapper and producer Sir Mix-a-Lot (born Anthony Ray) thinks about 1990s Seattle, he thinks about two music genres happening simultaneously: hip-hop and rock. As the '90s began, hip-hop was moving from more of a "home brew" sound to something "more polished." Mix and everyone he was working with at the time, including at his label Nastymix, had to step up their game, he says, since the songs were reaching far beyond the Emerald City bounds.

"I was coming off what I thought was a giant record," says Mix of his 1988 debut LP, *Swass*. "And we thought we had arrived!"

Mix's first album featured his first hit, "Posse on Broadway," as well as the local favorite, "Buttermilk Biscuits (Keep on Square Dancin')." His 1989 follow-up, *Seminar*, was certified gold, with songs like "Beepers" and "My Hooptie." Mix, however, is quick to note that around this same time, grunge music was also beginning to take off—in a major way. The lyricist knew it. "I felt like,

yeah, this is going to overshadow me. And it did!" he says.

Mix, however, wasn't frustrated that grunge was taking over in the late '80s and early '90s. Many of the musicians in the popular bands were his friends and collaborators. (Indeed, there remains an unreleased Mix and Chris Ballew collab.) "You could stand outside on Broadway and hear people rehearsing," says Mix. "It was quality band after quality band after quality band. Nobody sounded like shit. *Nobody*."

Born August 12, 1963, in Auburn, Mix grew up in Seattle's Central District. As a teen, via bussing programs many opposed at the time, Mix attended Roosevelt High School (at the same time as future Guns N' Roses bassist Duff McKagan). In middle school, Mix had been introduced to the idea of music as a career. He always loved electronics, from CB radios to keyboards, and in high school that crystallized.

As the '80s unspooled into the '90s, Mix started to notice the city changing. He was around members of groups like Pearl Jam and he remembers walking down the street and going into clubs and seeing musical giants onstage. At the time, it all felt, well, normal. In 1991, Mix signed with Def American Recordings, which boasted artists like Johnny Cash and ZZ Top, working with famed producer Rick Rubin.

"Then fast-forward to 1993 and we're all standing at the Grammys," says Mix. "Literally. Myself, the Presidents, Pearl Jam, everybody. It was that fast. Seattle took over."

The success of grunge made it a bit harder for hip-hop to be noticed, Mix says. Once 1992 came and went, it was all about sludgy rock. "You'd do a concert for, like, 3,000 people and then Pearl Jam shows up and plays for a stadium! But I wasn't jealous because all eyes were on Seattle."

In 1993, it was Mix's turn. While he recognizes he may not be the best rapper who ever lived—in Seattle, he credits the Emerald Street Boys, who came up before him, with that title—his unique combination of talent and style paid off that year. "Let's be honest," Mix says, "if the Emerald Street Boys came along around my time, as polished as they were, I'd have been sweeping up after them. That's how good they were."

Yet as the '90s progressed, rap grew and grew. Mix earned a Grammy in 1993 for his single "Baby Got Back." The song also hit No. 1 on the Billboard charts. He'd arrived. But he says that wasn't the song that the locals liked most. Those in Seattle liked "Posse on Broadway," "My Hooptie," and "Beepers" best. But as long as the people liked *something*, he says, and made sure to treat him like a human being, he was happy.

"Everybody was humble, thankfully," Mix says. "I could walk down the street and maybe somebody would buy me a Dick's burger. But there was no ass-kissing, which is what I like. Ass-kissing is very uncomfortable."

Today, what makes the city so unique for Mix is its location (read: isolation). He says the city and its residents historically had to come up with their own things to do. Their own fun. Their own music. That gave the region a unique sound and perspective. Seattle wasn't like anyplace else because it wasn't influenced by anyplace else. What Mix saw was a lot of people making art in odd, makeshift places. Working on stuff that was taboo. Not the glam stuff of the L.A. '80s.

"Grunge was not that," says Mix, famous for his signature cowboy hat. "It was like, 'I got some goddamn jeans on. I have an old guitar that I got when I was broke and I'm still playing it.' That was the beauty of it to me."

▲ Nirvana performing at an MTV taping at Pier 48, Seattle, 1993

OLETA ADAMS

SINGLE: "GET HERE"

RECORD: CIRCLE OF ONE

RELEASED: 1990 | **RECORDED IN:** BOX, ENGLAND

PRODUCER: ROLAND ORZABAL, DAVID BASCOMBE

LABEL: FONTANA RECORDS

Daughter of a preacher, powerhouse singer Oleta Adams was born in Seattle and later moved east with her family to Yakima, Washington. She was performing at the Peppercorn Duck Club in Kansas City in 1985 when she was discovered by Roland Orzabal and Curt Smith of the British pop-rock band Tears for Fears. Two years later, the group contacted her about joining them for the recording of their forthcoming album *Seeds of Love*. She plays piano and sings on the platinum-selling LP.

After the successful release of *Seeds of Love*, Tears for Fears' label Fontana Records offered Adams a recording contract, and Orzabal and David Bascombe produced her third solo LP, *Circle of One*. That album includes the soaring cover of the 1988 single "Get Here" by Brenda Russell. In 1991,

Circle of One peaked at No. 1 on the UK albums chart, thanks to the song's success, which earned Adams a Grammy nomination. Adams's follow-up in 1993, *Evolution*, also charted in the UK.

Adams is also the featured vocalist on the Billboard-charting single "Woman in Chains," a Tears for Fears song that featured iconic artist Phil Collins on drums; she later toured with Collins in 1998. Adams has released ten albums to date—her latest was *Third Set* in 2017—along with two compilation records. She has been nominated for several awards, including four Grammys.

KID SENSATION

SINGLE: "PRISONER OF IGNORANCE"

RECORD: ROLLIN' WITH NUMBER ONE

RELEASED: 1990 | **RECORDED IN:** SEATTLE

PRODUCER: DJ SKILL, KID SENSATION | **LABEL:** NASTYMIX RECORDS

Born Stephen Spence in 1971 in Seattle, rapper Kid Sensation (who later went by the name Xola Malik) made his debut as a guest emcee on the song "Rippn" from Sir Mix-a-Lot's 1988 album, *Swass*. He has since racked up an impressive resume, selling over one million records during his career and hosting the popular television shows *Yo! MTV Raps* and BET's *Rap City*. He released his debut album, *Rollin' with Number One*, in July of 1990.

The LP includes acclaimed tracks like "Back to Boom," "Seatown Ballers," and "Prisoner of Ignorance." At one point along the way, Kid Sensation met Seattle Mariners baseball legend Ken Griffey Jr. The two developed a friendship, and Griffey features as a rhymer on one of the rapper's hits—the 1992 song "The Way I Swing."

Rollin' with Number One includes the brilliant track "Prisoner of Ignorance," which tells the story of a young person dealing with the everyday struggle of life

as a Black American. The young person must
navigate a society that devalues his very
existence. Everything snowballs into a life
of crime, and he becomes a suspect for an
armed robbery gone bad.

One of the most powerful takeaways from this
song is the message Kid Sensation delivers
about the hardships young people of color
face daily, from discrimination in the classroom to the terror felt by the presence of
the police. The song takes listeners on a
journey from birth to death row. Had America
treated the protagonist differently, all could
have been avoided. This song alone cements
Kid Sensation's legacy as one of Seattle's
expert storytellers.

MOTHER LOVE BONE

SINGLE: "CROWN OF THORNS"

RECORD: APPLE

RELEASED: 1990 | **RECORDED IN:** SEATTLE; SAUSALITO, CA

PRODUCER: BRUCE CALDER, TERRY DATE, MARK DEARNLEY, MOTHER LOVE BONE

LABEL: STARDOG/MERCURY

Fronted by Andrew Wood, a singer with Fabio-like handsomeness and wheelbarrows of personality, Mother Love Bone was the precursor to the grunge revolution. Wood, who previously fronted the local band Malfunkshun, was its star. That is, until Wood and the band became a tragic casualty of the musical movement.

With an expressive, dynamic voice, the singer (a former roommate of Chris Cornell) shines on the song "Crown of Thorns," from the group's studio debut, *Apple*. On it, Wood, nicknamed "Landrew the Love Child," displays an elastic voice, golden and reminiscent of Guns N' Roses frontman Axl Rose. The band—comprised of Wood, guitarist Bruce Fairweather, drummer Greg Gilmore, and Pearl Jam guitarist Stone Gossard and bassist Jeff Ament—was one part glam,

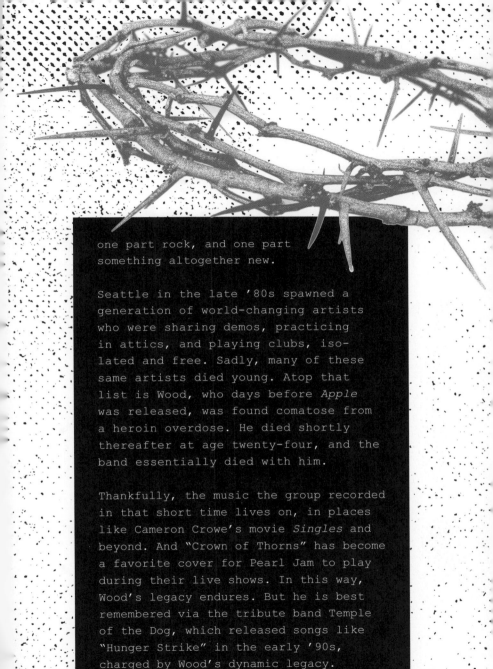

one part rock, and one part
something altogether new.

Seattle in the late '80s spawned a
generation of world-changing artists
who were sharing demos, practicing
in attics, and playing clubs, isolated and free. Sadly, many of these
same artists died young. Atop that
list is Wood, who days before *Apple*
was released, was found comatose from
a heroin overdose. He died shortly
thereafter at age twenty-four, and the
band essentially died with him.

Thankfully, the music the group recorded
in that short time lives on, in places
like Cameron Crowe's movie *Singles* and
beyond. And "Crown of Thorns" has become
a favorite cover for Pearl Jam to play
during their live shows. In this way,
Wood's legacy endures. But he is best
remembered via the tribute band Temple
of the Dog, which released songs like
"Hunger Strike" in the early '90s,
charged by Wood's dynamic legacy.

QUEENSRŸCHE

SINGLE: "SILENT LUCIDITY"

RECORD: EMPIRE

RELEASED: 1990 | **RECORDED IN:** REDMOND, WA; VANCOUVER, BC

PRODUCER: PETER COLLINS | **LABEL:** EMI

Beginning with a bright, staccato acoustic, the nearly-six-minute "Silent Lucidity" blossoms with somber, David Bowie-esque vocals from frontman Geoff Tate, and progresses into guitar solos and cymbal crashes. From the Bellevue-born prog rock band's 1990 LP *Empire*, the song soars, a wedge of seagulls in the bright blue sky. The track was also Queensrÿche's most successful song, hitting No. 1 on the Billboard Mainstream Rock Songs chart and No. 9 on the Hot 100. The triple-platinum album was critically lauded as well, earning the band Grammy nominations.

Originally including Tate, drummer Scott Rockenfield, bassist Eddie Jackson, and guitar players Michael Wilton and Chris DeGarmo, Queensrÿche boasts sixteen studio LPs and is widely considered one of the three founders of prog rock, along with Fates Warning and Dream Theater. The band is part of a lineage of heavy metal groups from the region, which date as far back as the '70s and include bands like Metal Church.

More recently, though, Queensrÿche has experienced some tension. After a blowup backstage in Brazil in 2012, Tate was fired from the band. He and his wife, Susan, Queensrÿche's then manager, sued the group for wrongful termination. In the interim years before a judgment was levied, the remaining members and Tate were allowed to tour independently using the band moniker.

In 2013, Tate, under the name Geoff Tate's Queensrÿche, put out the album *Frequency Unknown*. And today Queensrÿche officially includes Wilton and Jackson, along with drummer Casey Grillo, guitarist Mike Stone, and singer Todd La Torre. Whatever form the lineups take, their head-whipping rock memory lives on.

HAMMERBOX

SINGLE: "WHEN 3 IS 2"

RECORD: HAMMERBOX

RELEASED: 1991 | **RECORDED IN:** SHORELINE, WA; SEATTLE

PRODUCER: HAMMERBOX, ED BROOKS | **LABEL:** C/Z RECORDS

The buzzing rock group Hammerbox formed in Seattle in 1990. Fronted by vocalist Carrie Akre, the band included guitarist Harris Thurmond, bassist James Atkins, and drummer Dave Birenbaum. The group released its debut self-titled LP in 1991, which led Hammerbox to sign with the prestigious A&M Records in 1993 for the release of its second studio LP, *Numb*. Sadly, for fans of the cutting-edge group, Hammerbox dissolved in 1994. But Akre went on to form Goodness, which included the likes of local rockers Danny Newcomb and Chris Friel. Akre is also the frontwoman for the current Seattle supergroup the Rockfords, which includes lead guitarist Mike McCready.

After Hammerbox disbanded, Thurmond joined the group Anodyne before forming several other projects. Though Hammerbox was a short-lived phenomenon, their impact is no less significant. Their single "When 3 Is 2," from the group's

debut LP, showcases an early grunge
sound with a stalwart female vocalist,
giving Seattle its answer to groups like
Garbage and the Cranberries. But more
than that, Hammerbox was blessed with
a quintessential PNW sound—the wall of
guitar music seemingly filtered through
chilled evergreens and sharpened by
mountain peaks. Indeed, with Akre front
and center, Hammerbox was a fierce force
of nature.

TAD

SINGLE: "JACK PEPSI"

RECORD: 8-WAY SANTA

RELEASED: 1991 | **RECORDED IN:** MADISON, WI

PRODUCER: BUTCH VIG | **LABEL:** SUB POP RECORDS

Music producer Butch Vig is one of the unsung heroes of '90s rock, producing Nirvana's *Nevermind* and performing with and producing Garbage. He also led the charge on the 1991 hard-rock record *8-Way Santa*, from the Seattle-born group Tad. Founded by Thomas Andrew Doyle, the band was one of the first signed to the then-burgeoning Sub Pop label. Tad was also one of the first bands to usher in the grunge genre.

Formed in 1988, the group included former Skin Yard drummer Steve Wied, bassist Kurt Danielson, and guitarist Gary Thorstensen. As many early Sub Pop acts did, Tad recorded with "Grungefather" Jack Endino. The group released its debut LP in early 1989, and after a European tour with Nirvana, they recorded *8-Way Santa*, their third LP. The record includes the sludgy single "Jack Pepsi," which caused the soft drink company to sue the band for releasing the song using the Pepsi logo (oops!). Tad garnered another lawsuit for their third LP. The cover, a found photo of a man touching a woman's breast, brought controversy when the woman, who became a born-again Christian and remarried, sued and Sub Pop was forced to change the cover. The album also featured the song "Jinx," which was used in the 1992 film *Singles*.

Tad released its major label debut *Inhaler* in 1993 and spent time touring and opening for Soundgarden the following year. Afterward, the band released a few more records, but it dissolved in 1999, never quite breaking through to the mainstream. The grunge group got back together for a few shows, and Doyle released his latest solo album, *Forgotten Sciences*, in 2023.

TEMPLE OF THE DOG

SINGLE: "HUNGER STRIKE"

RECORD: TEMPLE OF THE DOG

RELEASED: 1991 | **RECORDED IN:** SEATTLE

PRODUCER: RICK PARASHAR, TEMPLE OF THE DOG

LABEL: A&M RECORDS

Founded in the wake of musician Andy Wood's death, Temple of the Dog was spearheaded by the grunge musician's former roommate, Soundgarden frontman Chris Cornell. In one respect, Temple of the Dog is a supergroup. In another, it's a collection of Wood's closest friends mourning his loss, from Cornell and Soundgarden drummer Matt Cameron to Pearl Jam members Mike McCready, Eddie Vedder, Jeff Ament, and Stone Gossard (the latter two were in Wood's band, Mother Love Bone). Also in 1991, Pearl Jam released its debut LP, *Ten*, just four months before Temple of the Dog released its sole studio LP.

Recorded in Seattle's London Bridge Studio, Temple of the Dog's self-titled album was not initially popular. But it would gain fame as the grunge rock movement rose to prominence in the mid-1990s. The band's self-titled LP has since been certified platinum. Members later reunited in 2016 to celebrate the twenty-fifth anniversary of their LP, the band's only tour. Temple of the Dog is also one of several other local super-groups. Another is Mad Season, which featured McCready on guitar, Screaming Trees drummer Barrett Martin, Alice in Chains vocalist Layne Staley, and John Baker Saunders on bass. That band released its sole LP, *Above*, in 1995.

But in 1990 when Wood died of a heroin overdose, Cornell, who was in between tours with Soundgarden, began writing music as a tribute to his fallen friend. One of those songs was the hit "Say Hello 2 Heaven." These tunes began to spawn more music and soon members of the band found themselves in the recording studio, wanting to release an entire album to commemorate Wood. Vedder, in Seattle in 1990 to audition for the group that would become Pearl Jam, lent his vocals to various tracks, including "Hunger Strike," a duet with Cornell. This became the first single released, and "Hunger Strike" became the band's most popular track. The song has since been covered by Pearl Jam, the rocker Daughtry, and more.

PEARL JAM

SINGLE: "ALIVE"

RECORD: TEN

RELEASED: 1991 | **RECORDED IN:** SEATTLE; SURREY, ENGLAND

PRODUCER: RICK PARASHAR, PEARL JAM | **LABEL:** EPIC

The story of Pearl Jam begins with many disparate, moving parts. Formed in Seattle in 1990, the band started to come together first with members of Green River, a rock group that included Stone Gossard and Jeff Ament (and future Mudhoney lead singer Mark Arm). Gossard and Ament played in Mother Love Bone before that group tragically dissolved after the death of its frontman, Andrew Wood. In the wake of that loss, Gossard began to jam with another Seattle standout, guitarist Mike McCready, whose band Shadow had just broken up. Gossard and McCready reconnected with Ament and, together, looked for a drummer.

During that search, the trio connected with former Red Hot Chili Peppers kit player Jack Irons, who declined the offer but introduced them to San Diego singer Eddie Vedder, then a gas station attendant. Vedder listened to an early demo tape from Pearl Jam, which included the songs "Alive" and "Once." After going surfing, Vedder recorded some lyrics and sent the tape back to Seattle. Impressed, Gossard, Ament, and McCready met the singer in town later for an audition, during which time Vedder recorded vocals for Temple of the Dog.

Vedder was officially in. Next, the band recruited drummer Dave Krusen, one of many drummers Pearl Jam would include during its history. The group also settled on its first moniker: Mookie Blaylock, after an NBA point guard known for his defense. Within a month of playing its first show, Mookie Blaylock was opening for Alice in Chains.

Later, with the name changed to Pearl Jam—a nod to Vedder's great-grandmother and to the "jam" music played by the likes of Neil Young—the quintet put out its debut 11-track LP, *Ten*, in 1991. That album, along with others from groups like Soundgarden, Nirvana, and Alice in Chains, was foundational to the grunge revolution of the 1990s. Today, "Alive," which was one of the group's first songs, showcases Vedder's booming voice, McCready's shredding, and all the musicians' knack for epic rock songs that can shake the globe. The song, which hit No. 16 on the Billboard Mainstream Rock Songs chart, remains a fan favorite. To date, Pearl Jam has released a dozen studio LPs, along with many more live records and bootlegs.

NIRVANA

SINGLE: "SMELLS LIKE TEEN SPIRIT"

RECORD: NEVERMIND

RELEASED: 1991 | **RECORDED IN:** LOS ANGELES; MADISON, WI

PRODUCER: BUTCH VIG | **LABEL:** DGC

If Seattle had to pick one song to represent it for the rest of time, locals would likely vote for the track "Smells Like Teen Spirit." The song features one of the city's most famous artists, Kurt Cobain, along with a rampaging rock sound. It's a nod to both Seattle's musical past and its promising musical future. The single is also perhaps the most famous grunge song ever, prized in a city that was in many ways put on the musical map because of the sludgy, emotive sound.

Formed in Aberdeen, Washington, Nirvana first consisted of Cobain and close friend and bassist Krist Novoselic. Like Pearl Jam, Nirvana struggled to find a permanent drummer before landing on then-DC-based Dave Grohl (who would later, after Cobain's death, form Foo Fighters). Nirvana recorded its first album, *Bleach*, with "Grungefather" engineer Jack Endino and released it in 1989 via the new Pacific Northwest-based label Sub Pop Records.

The success of that album, coupled with Cobain's artistry and commanding stage presence, led to more popularity, which in turn led to the band's sophomore album, *Nevermind*, recorded in spring of 1991 and released that fall. The result? Explosive fame, the kind that pushed Cobain further into his addictions and later into taking his own life. The album opens with "Smells Like Teen Spirit," a track that many have claimed was the voice of a new generation. The song was all over the radio and its music video all over MTV. "I was trying to write the ultimate pop song," Cobain told *Rolling Stone* in 1994. At first, the band dismissed the track as trite but eventually found its groove and recorded it during the *Nevermind* sessions. The song title was inspired by a quip from riot grrrl icon and Cobain's friend Kathleen Hanna, who wrote on Cobain's bedroom wall one day, "Kurt smells like Teen Spirit." At the time, Teen Spirit was a type of deodorant.

The (ironic) success of the anti-establishment *Nevermind* caused the band members to recede from the spotlight at times, and Cobain eventually retreated to an apartment in Seattle, with a severe heroin addiction. In 1993, the band recorded its third studio LP, *In Utero*, but Cobain died the next year on April 5 at just twenty-seven years old. He was survived by his wife, famed rocker Courtney Love, and their child, Frances Bean Cobain. As for "Smells Like Teen Spirit," the song hit No. 1 on myriad charts in a number of different countries, from Australia to Spain, and it remains as well-known and well-regarded today as it was upon its initial release.

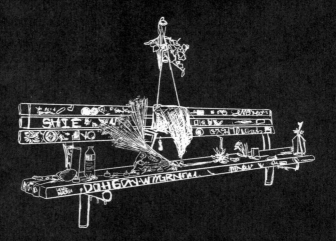

KURT
COBAIN
HAUNTS

MEMORIAL BENCH
151 LAKE WASHINGTON
BOULEVARD E, SEATTLE

There are dozens of locations in Seattle and Cobain's hometown of Aberdeen that fans of the artist can visit if they want to stand in the same space where the Nirvana frontman once frequented. There's where he was last seen in public (Linda's Tavern) or the home he grew up in (1210 East 1st Street in Aberdeen). There's a bench in Viretta Park (151 Lake Washington Boulevard East in Seattle) near where he was found dead in his final home that is now decorated with lyrics in a lovely makeshift memorial.

There's the less-than-five-star Marco Polo Motel, where Cobain would hide out in town, often in room 226. Truly, if you walk around the city with someone who knows Cobain's life story, they will point out a string of places in neighborhoods like Capitol Hill where Cobain was known to busk with an old acoustic guitar. Or another where he panhandled for change to get a meal.

There are also the clubs, bars, and venues he's famous for playing in the city, from Central Saloon in Pioneer Square, which was home to Nirvana's first Seattle show, to the Crocodile Café, which has since moved from its original location, where Cobain crowd-surfed, tossing his guitar into the crowd's open hands. And the beloved (though now defunct) dive, Re-bar, where Nirvana played their *Nevermind* release show— amazingly, the band was kicked out of the venue that night after the set.

There's also the ornate, palatial 3,000-person theater, the Paramount, where Nirvana played for feverish fans and later provided footage for a concert film, *Live at the Paramount*. Or there's Robert Lang Studios, a favorite of grunge bands like Alice in Chains, with its secret doors and catacomb rooms, where Nirvana recorded several songs that would become posthumous hits. Indeed, Cobain's ghost is still felt all over Seattle, the city and the artist forever intertwined.

LOVE BATTERY

SINGLE: "OUT OF FOCUS"

RECORD: DAYGLO

RELEASED: 1992 | **RECORDED IN:** SEATTLE

PRODUCER: CONRAD UNO, JOHN AUER | **LABEL:** SUB POP RECORDS

Born in Seattle in 1989, Love Battery named itself after a song from the UK band the Buzzcocks. The group's original lineup included Ron Nine of the band Room Nine, former Crisis Party guitarist Kevin Whitworth and bassist Tommy Simpson, and Mudhoney drummer Dan Peters. Peters, though, left Love Battery before the group released its first single and was replaced by former Skin Yard drummer Jason Finn, later of the Presidents of the United States of America. Before the release of their second LP, *Dayglo*, Simpson also left the band and was replaced by ex-U-Men bassist Jim Tillman. Got all that? Good!

When Love Battery released its first full-length album, the band was signed to prestigious local label Sub Pop. As a collective, Love Battery was a standout act with their bent of psychedelic sounds, a contrast to their peers during the grunge revolution. "Out of Focus," the most recognized track on the album, is introduced with distorted guitar strums and feedback that leads into a wall of guitar sound with a heavy, driving kickdrum. This propels the song forward, working

with the snare and a mesmerizing bass line that,
when played all together, keeps the listener in
a trance for the duration, long after Nine has
stopped singing. The result is among the city's
finest psychedelia-hard rock.

While members of the band came and went over the
years, the original *Dayglo* lineup reunited in
2018 to perform the record in its entirety for a
handful of Seattle shows. And a few years later,
Dayglo was remastered and reissued on vinyl via
Jackpot, keeping the legend of Love Battery alive.
One could say it just keeps going . . . and going
. . . and going . . .

SIR MIX-A-LOT

SINGLE: "BABY GOT BACK"

RECORD: MACK DADDY

RELEASED: 1992 | **RECORDED IN:** AUBURN, WA

PRODUCER: SIR MIX-A-LOT, RICK RUBIN, NATE FOX, STRANGE

LABEL: DEF AMERICAN, RHYME CARTEL RECORDS

Where would Seattle's music scene be without Sir Mix-a-Lot? The artist (born Anthony Ray) has been giving the area hip-hop credibility ever since the late 1980s with his debut album, *Swass*, and the hit song "Posse on Broadway." But it was Mix's third album that changed his life and turned him into a chart-topping, Grammy Award–winning musician. The 1992 LP *Mack Daddy* features the now iconic song "Baby Got Back." The track remains a favorite in karaoke bars and in television commercials today.

But what the song did, at its core, was normalize and celebrate people of different body types. Sure, it's fun to sing about butts. But what's more impressive is Mix's message of bringing people with curves into the spotlight—especially Black women, who were often neglected in media. Mix, who was born on August 12, 1963 in Auburn, recorded *Mack Daddy* in his hometown. He collaborated with famed producer, Rick Rubin, who suggested he speed up "Baby Got Back" from its original slower tempo. Mix agreed and the rest is history.

As a kid, Mix was bussed to Seattle's Roosevelt High School, where future Guns N' Roses bassist Duff McKagan was also a student, at a time when the school system was undertaking integration. In school, Mix began to consider the possibility of a career in music. Someone who had always loved gadgets and electronics, Mix started DJing after high school in the early '80s.

Years later, in 1992, while Mix was on a tour bus in Panama City, Florida, he found out "Baby Got Back" hit No. 1 on the Billboard Hot 100 as fans leaned from hotel room windows to cheer his arrival that night. Meanwhile, the music video for the song received "many, many complaints," said MTV. But that was the point, and why it became the second bestselling song in the United States in 1992. Later, bodacious rapper Nicki Minaj sampled the track in an even more salacious song and music video for "Anaconda."

Over the years, Mix has collaborated with local standouts like Mudhoney and the Presidents of the United States of America on music. He recorded Ayron Jones's debut LP and he passed Seattle's King of Rap torch to Macklemore as "Thrift Shop" blew up. Mix, however, will always remain the city's musical mayor.

DICK'S DRIVE-IN
115 BROADWAY E, SEATTLE

In 1988, Seattle rap icon Sir Mix-a-Lot released his first hit single, "Posse on Broadway." The classic hip-hop track, which came from Mix's debut album, *Swass*, helped make the quick-tongued rapper famous. And it led to him signing with Def Jam, working with Rick Rubin, and releasing the timeless classic "Baby Got Back."

In Mix's early hit, the lyricist talks about spending a night driving around the city with his friends. He describes the people they meet, their escapades. And he talks about one of the city's main streets.

Broadway, a main thoroughfare that cuts through the popular Capitol Hill neighborhood, itself is halved by Dick's Drive-In, a classic paper-hat burger joint that keeps its prices low, its lines moving, and its neighbors fed and happy. In the "Posse on Broadway" video, Mix and pals pull up to Dick's, the parking lot packed. Mix, a storyteller from the get-go, tells the tale of an altercation and helping a woman escape from an abusive date, rhyming crisply on the beat.

Fast-forward twenty-five years and Mix's Seattle hip-hop heirs Macklemore & Ryan Lewis (M&RL) paid homage to their forefather, shutting down Broadway one warm July 24 night. Shooting the music video

for the song "White Walls," M&RL, along with singer Hollis Wong-Wear, got to the top of the burger joint on Broadway and performed to thousands of onlooking fans, who had heard about the leaked shoot. Broadway had to be shut down for all foot traffic. It felt like all of Seattle was on Broadway that night.

Founded by Dick Spady in 1954, Dick's Drive-Ins are peppered throughout the Seattle area with just shy of a dozen locations, from Wallingford to Capitol Hill, Lake City, Queen Anne, Kent, Bellevue, and beyond. The place is famous for its quick service, minimal menu (always get the tartar sauce with your fries), and reliable food. Only recently did Dick's even start taking credit cards—it's that kind of old-fashioned place. And the most famous of them all is the Broadway location, now a historical hip-hop landmark.

SCREAMING TREES

SINGLE: "NEARLY LOST YOU"

RECORD: SWEET OBLIVION

RELEASED: 1992 | **RECORDED IN:** NEW YORK CITY

PRODUCER: DON FLEMING | **LABEL:** EPIC

The Mount Rushmore of grunge bands in Seattle would have to include Pearl Jam, Nirvana, Soundgarden, and Alice in Chains. But if we were to add a fifth, it would be Screaming Trees. Founded in rural Ellensburg, Washington, the band was fronted by low, gravelly-voiced singer Mark Lanegan, who sadly passed away in February of 2022 after a brutal bout with COVID-19. The group also included drummer Mark Pickerel, replaced in 1991 by iconic Seattle musician Barrett Martin, and brothers Gary Lee and Van Conner on guitar and bass.

The band's biggest hit, and the sole single to go platinum, was the song, "Nearly Lost You," which peaked at No. 12 on the Billboard Mainstream Rock Songs chart and was also included on the soundtrack for the popular 1992 Seattle-based film *Singles*, directed by Cameron Crowe (who was married to Heart's Nancy Wilson for a number of years). That soundtrack also included songs from Alice in Chains, Soundgarden, and Pearl Jam. "Nearly Lost You" was the first single released from Screaming Trees' sixth LP, *Sweet Oblivion*,

and it showcases the relentless-yet-forlorn sensibility that made them so famous.

Screaming Trees broke up in 2000 and, afterward, Lanegan enjoyed a fruitful solo career, playing with local standouts like Jeff Fielder. He was also a member of the bands Queens of the Stone Age and Mad Season. In 1990, Lanegan and Nirvana's Kurt Cobain recorded an album of Lead Belly songs. And in 2020, at the request of friend Anthony Bourdain, Lanegan released his memoir, *Sing Backwards and Weep*. Screaming Trees released ten albums, including their final LP, *Last Words: Final Recordings* in 2011.

ALICE IN CHAINS

SINGLE: "ROOSTER"

RECORD: DIRT

RELEASED: 1992 | **RECORDED IN:** BURBANK, CA; SEATTLE; LOS ANGELES

PRODUCER: DAVE JERDEN, ALICE IN CHAINS | **LABEL:** COLUMBIA

Of the biggest bands of the '90s in Seattle, many were fronted by just one person. Pearl Jam with Eddie Vedder, Nirvana with Kurt Cobain, Soundgarden with Chris Cornell. But Alice in Chains, the fourth of the Emerald City's "big four" grunge acts, boasted two singers: the somber Jerry Cantrell and electrifying Layne Staley. While the group released well-known albums, songs, and arguably the best *MTV Unplugged* performance (neck and neck with Nirvana), perhaps the group's most famous offering is the heavy song "Rooster."

The track, from the band's five-time platinum 1992 album *Dirt*, was written by Cantrell for his father, a US Army Vietnam veteran. The title of the track, which peaked at No. 7 on the Billboard Mainstream Rock Songs chart, came from Jerry Sr.'s childhood nickname, given to him by his great-grandfather. Cantrell wrote the song in 1991 while living in Seattle with Cornell and the Soundgarden singer's then-wife, Susan Silver. It's sung from the perspective of the former army man, highlighting the mental scars he accumulated as a result of the war. Cantrell later talked about how the track helped heal a fraught relationship with his father. Growing up, he and his family left his father, with the musician later saying in a 2006 interview, "It was an environment that wasn't good for anyone, so we took off to live with my grandmother in Washington."

Dirt—recorded in part in Los Angeles during the Rodney King riots—also included hit songs like "Would?" and "Down in a Hole." As with most of the grunge bands from Seattle, Alice in Chains dealt with tragedy when Staley passed away on April 5, 2002. Considered one of the greatest singers of his generation, the musician was just thirty-four years old. (Coincidently, April 5 is also the day Cobain died in 1994. It's also Pearl Jam guitarist Mike McCready's birthday.) Today, Alice in Chains is still recording and touring, filling the hole created by Staley's death with standout vocalist William DuVall. Rounding out the band is drummer Sean Kinney and bassist Mike Inez, who replaced former bassist Mike Starr. The group, which has garnered eleven Grammy Awards and five No. 1 songs, has released six studio LPs, including *Rainier Fog* in 2018.

KENNY G

SINGLE: "FOREVER IN LOVE"

RECORD: BREATHLESS

RELEASED: 1992 | **RECORDED IN:** SEATTLE; NEW YORK CITY;

SAUSALITO, CA; LOS ANGELES

PRODUCER: KENNY G, WALTER AFANASIEFF, DAVID FOSTER, DAN SHEA

LABEL: ARISTA

One of the bestselling artists of all time, Kenneth Bruce Gorelick—a.k.a. Kenny G—was born in Seattle on June 5, 1956. The face of "smooth jazz," a genre he essentially invented, Kenny G is known for playing his alto saxophone in ways that calm and mesmerize. (For others in the area who write similar meditative music, check out Bellingham's Soundings of the Planet.) When Kenny G released his 1986 album *Duotones*, the artist was immediately put on the map. To date, he's sold more than seventy-five million albums.

Kenny G, who first noticed the saxophone as a kid while watching *The Ed Sullivan Show*, began play-ing it when he was just ten years old. Later, he attended Franklin High School and then the University of Washington. His first major gig was playing in Barry White's Love Unlimited Orchestra in 1973 at age seventeen. Around that time, he also played in the Seattle funk band, Cold, Bold & Together. In 1982, he signed to Arista as a solo artist after recording his self-titled solo album the year prior. His following two records, *G Force* and *Gravity*, both went platinum. His 1986 album, *Duotones*, sold more than five million copies in the United States. In 1992, he released *Breathless*, which became the bestselling instrumental album ever, selling some fifteen million copies worldwide and hitting No. 2 on the Billboard 200. It remains one of the top 100 bestselling albums ever in the United States for its universal sense of calm.

But the oft-criticized musician has remained polarizing, with critics saying his sound is bereft of any real artistic soul, especially for someone who calls himself a jazz musician. But Kenny G has always been able to wave away any negativity; he's even able to joke about it. In 1997, the musician earned a *Guinness Book of World Records* nod for playing the longest-held note ever on a saxophone, playing an E-flat for 45 minutes and 47 seconds thanks to "circular breathing." His song "Forever in Love," from *Breathless*, was released in 1992 and it subsequently hit No. 1 on the US and Canada adult contemporary charts, earning him a Grammy for Best Instrumental Composition at the 1994 show. It's a somber, reflective, digestible tune, as docile as it is intricate. These days, Kenny G is still recording and releasing albums, including his 2021 LP, *New Standards*.

MUDHONEY

SINGLE: "SUCK YOU DRY"

RECORD: PIECE OF CAKE

RELEASED: 1992 | **RECORDED IN:** SEATTLE

PRODUCER: CONRAD UNO, MUDHONEY | **LABEL:** REPRISE RECORDS

It's often the case that the people who create something new don't get the credit those who later perfect or promulgate it do. In many ways, this is true for the rock band known as Mudhoney. While the group formed in Seattle in 1988, its roots go much deeper. Originally, frontman Mark McLaughlin (a.k.a. Mark Arm) started a band called Mr. Epp and the Calculations around 1978 in the Seattle suburb of Bellevue, naming the band after his math teacher. The group played its first real show in 1981, releasing an EP in 1983, and played its final show in 1984 with Malfunkshun, an early grunge group fronted by Andrew Wood.

Later that year, Arm and company formed Green River, which included future Pearl Jam members Jeff Ament and Stone Gossard. Green River's 1985 debut EP, *Come on Down*, is considered the first-ever grunge album. But when Green River broke up, Ament and Gossard joined Mother Love Bone with Wood.

And that brings us to 1988, when Arm cofounded Mudhoney, the moniker taken from the Russ Meyer movie. At its outset, the band included Arm, guitarist Steve Turner, drummer Dan Peters, and bassist Matt Lukin (formerly of Melvins), who was later replaced by Guy Maddison. The group released its debut EP, *Superfuzz Bigmuff*, for Sub Pop, which included the hit "Touch Me I'm Sick." They released their self-titled LP in 1989. Instantly, Mudhoney became the face of Sub Pop, beloved by bands from Sonic Youth to Nirvana. In 1992, the group signed with Reprise Records and released *Piece of Cake*. Their song "Overblown" was also featured on the soundtrack for the 1992 film *Singles*.

"Suck You Dry" is a wailing, hard-rock track that showcases Arm's pounding vocals. Not overly melodic, not overly flamboyant, Arm lands a power punch . . . like a guitar chord about to blow out a speaker. The song hit No. 23 on the Billboard Modern Rock Tracks chart, and *Piece of Cake* hit No. 9 on the Heatseekers Albums chart. Tracked at Egg Studios in Seattle, the record is one of a dozen recorded by the band, includ-ing *Plastic Eternity*, which dropped in 2023.

THE GITS

SINGLE: "SECOND SKIN"

RECORD: FRENCHING THE BULLY

RELEASED: 1992 | **RECORDED IN:** SEATTLE

PRODUCER: SCOTT BENSON, STEVE FISK | **LABEL:** C/Z RECORDS

While punk rock band the Gits formed in Ohio at Antioch College in 1986, the group set down roots in Seattle in the early '90s. It was led by vocalist Mia Zapata. But as many locals know, Zapata was brutally raped and killed one night in 1993 after leaving Comet Tavern in Capitol Hill, where she worked as a bartender. What made matters worse, the case wasn't solved for ten years. Zapata had been a fixture in the local music scene. Tragically, she never got to see the fruits of her labor.

Not a grunge band and not formally part of the riot grrrl movement, the Gits were nevertheless significant in many ways in the Seattle music scene. The Gits released their debut LP, *Frenching the Bully*, in 1992; it included the ferocious track "Second Skin" (originally released as a single in 1991), a song about needing more protection and something tough to keep Zapata safe. In 1994, after her death, the band released the posthumous sophomore LP *Enter: The Conquering Chicken*, which included a blues-rock rendition of Sam Cooke's "A Change Is Gonna Come."

Even though the band never made it big, it likely could have. In fact, music biz professional Tom Sommer has said he was set to sign the band to Atlantic Records, even shaking hands with the members just four days before Zapata died. Sommer wrote in the British outlet the *Observer*, "Four days after shaking hands with the Gits on a deal, Mia Zapata was murdered. As anyone who was an active part of the Seattle scene in the early '90s can tell you, this tragedy may have been more of a blow to the city than Kurt Cobain's death." Sommer also called Zapata "the best female vocalist of her generation." We can only be thankful that her early work lives on.

CANDLEBOX

SINGLE: "FAR BEHIND"

RECORD: CANDLEBOX

RELEASED: 1993 | **RECORDED IN:** SEATTLE

PRODUCER: KELLY GRAY, CANDLEBOX | **LABEL:** MAVERICK

With its familiar, reflective electric-guitar opening riff and heavy, crashing vocals from frontman Kevin Martin, "Far Behind" is one of the most memorable tracks from the 1990s rock catalog. Seattle-born Candlebox formed in 1990 and released its self-titled LP in the summer of 1993. That album features "Far Behind" and "You," which peaked at No. 18 and No. 78 on the Billboard Hot 100, respectively. The album was subsequently certified four-times platinum. Its follow-up LP, *Lucy*, was certified gold. In total, Candlebox, comprised originally of Martin, guitarist Peter Klett, bassist Bardi Martin, and drummer Scott Mercado, has released eight LPs.

The first successful band on Maverick, a label that would later feature Alanis Morissette and the Prodigy, Candlebox would go on to tour with groups like the Offspring, Aerosmith, Radiohead, and the Flaming Lips. "Far Behind" was written as a tribute for the late grunge icon Andrew Wood. In a 1994 interview, Martin said the song "represents the loss of love between friends and having to be left with the feeling of emptiness."

He added in a 1998 interview, "I wrote 'Far Behind' for Andy Wood." As for the album on which the track appears, *Candlebox* was recorded at two iconic Seattle studios, London Bridge and Robert Lang. Today, the LP is remembered for breaking the group into the spotlight and for its remembrance of Wood—"Far Behind" continues to evoke those thoughts as soon as you hear the echoing guitar riff that kicks off the track.

THE FASTBACKS

SINGLE: "GONE TO THE MOON"

RECORD: ZÜCKER

RELEASED: 1993 | **RECORDED IN:** SEATTLE

PRODUCER: KURT BLOCH | **LABEL:** SUB POP RECORDS

One of the benefits of Seattle's location in the upper-left corner of the United States is that it's isolated from the rest of the world. With an ocean to the west, the Canadian border to the north, and rural, rugged areas to the east and south, people didn't routinely mess with the city much until the tech boom invasion around the turn of the twenty-first century. As such, bands could do, say, and create the music they wanted. For example: punk rock band the Fastbacks, fronted by local music legend Kurt Bloch and founded in 1979. The band, which also included guitarist Lulu Gargiulo and bassist Kim Warnick (later of Visqueen), stuck around until 2001. (Bloch also played in the band the Young Fresh Fellows, known for their humorous song "Amy Grant.")

Throughout the Fastbacks' tenure, the band cycled through many drummers, including Duff McKagan, who would later earn fame as the bassist for Guns N' Roses. Jason Finn, later of the Presidents of the United States of America, would play the kit too. Local drum hero Mike Musburger spent a lot of time

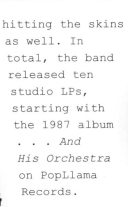

hitting the skins
as well. In
total, the band
released ten
studio LPs,
starting with
the 1987 album
. . . *And
His Orchestra*
on PopLlama
Records.

The group's
14-track 1993 LP,
Zücker, released on
the Sub Pop label, was
the band's most commer-
cially successful. It featured a cover of a
Bee Gees song "Please Read Me," as well as
the short but powerful "Gone to the Moon."
Rusty Willoughby played drums for this LP,
adding his name to the band's long roster.
"Gone to the Moon" even got its own music
video, which featured live footage and
shots of a 1950s-esque classroom with
paper airplanes and mathematical equa-
tions. The song is rambunctious and
punk, sticky and pop tinged.

MELVINS

SINGLE: "HONEY BUCKET"

RECORD: HOUDINI

RELEASED: 1993 | **RECORDED IN:** SAN FRANCISCO; SEATTLE

PRODUCER: MELVINS, KURT COBAIN, GGGARTH | **LABEL:** ATLANTIC RECORDS

Formed in 1983 in tiny, sparse Montesano, Washington, Melvins have been credited as a key factor in the development of grunge and sludge metal. The two consistent members of the group include guitarist and vocalist Buzz Osborne and drummer Dale Crover, while other members have come and gone. Osborne and Crover are the primary songwriters on the seminal album *Houdini*. Lorax (Lori Black) also received credit for playing bass—strangely, she didn't actually play on the album. Another fun fact: Lorax's mother is 1930s child screen star and later US ambassador Shirley Temple. Fans will notice another familiar name printed on the album's liner notes: Kurt Cobain. The Nirvana frontman was given a producer credit on the record. However, Cobain was fired from the project midstream, reportedly too difficult to work with according to Osborne. In the end, the LP marked the band's first release on Atlantic Records, and it became Melvins' biggest-selling record.

Melvins went on to inspire numerous groups, including Nirvana and Soundgarden. The fifth track on *Houdini*, "Honey Bucket," opens with three clicks of the drumsticks and is immediately followed by a heavy, driving electric guitar, which is soon joined by powerful, smacking drums, amplifying the group's raw force. It's Melvins' heavy metal and brooding, sludgy guitar sounds that have made the group one of your favorite rock band's favorite bands. For fans of the song, "Honey Bucket" is too short for its own good. Clocking in at three minutes, the song shows Melvins are just getting warmed up. If you listen to it on repeat, warm yourself up with a few head rolls, or else you might risk a head-banging injury.

BIKINI KILL

SINGLE: "REBEL GIRL"

RECORD: PUSSY WHIPPED

RELEASED: 1993 | **RECORDED IN:** SEATTLE

PRODUCER: STUART HALLERMAN | **LABEL:** KILL ROCK STARS

In the history of Seattle-area music, few movements are as significant as riot grrrl. The underground feminist punk effort, complete with its own manifesto, put women front of stage and said, really fucking loudly, that men weren't the only ones who could rock. Since its foundational days in Olympia, the ethos has grown, first to places like Washington, DC, and then internationally. While focused on centering women, it also fought against physical abuse, racism, homophobia, and the patriarchy and encouraged female empowerment via DIY concerts, talks, handmade zines, and more.

And no band was more important in the movement's history than Bikini Kill. (Other important local groups include Bratmobile, Heavens to Betsy, Excuse 17, and Sleater-Kinney.) Formed in Olympia in 1990 largely on the campus of the Evergreen State College, Bikini Kill included frontwoman Kathleen Hanna, guitarist Billy Karren, bassist Kathi Wilcox, and drummer Tobi Vail. Hanna, a friend of Nirvana's Kurt Cobain, has also been part of seminal bands like Le Tigre and the Julie Ruin. Today, she is still producing work,

including a 2024 memoir, *Rebel Girl: My Life as a Feminist Punk*, and touring. She is married to Beastie Boy Adam Horovitz.

Bikini Kill is a seminal riot grrrl band and its iconic empowering song "Rebel Girl" continues to resonate with original fans and legions of listeners discovering the band anew. The feminist punk song was released on the band's 12-track 1993 debut studio LP, *Pussy Whipped*, although it was performed live as early as 1991. A 7-inch single of "Rebel Girl" was even produced by iconic rocker Joan Jett. It's an anthem for female power and a call for more to follow suit. The unabashed song has since been an inspiration to many, from Green Day's Billie Joe Armstrong to burgeoning punk rock group, the Linda Lindas.

A NOTE ON
RIOT GRRRL

The underground feminist punk movement riot grrrl began in the Pacific Northwest in the early 1990s, specifically in the Washington State capital city of Olympia and its Evergreen State College. Since, the musical and creative effort—unafraid to challenge sexist conventions and express righteous anger in song—has expanded globally. Associated with third-wave feminism, the riot grrrl community saw many bands and artists fighting a common battle, addressing issues of violence against women, sexual discrimination, classism, and more. The movement also spread messages of female empowerment in song and written work.

Born out of the DIY (do-it-yourself) scene in the Northwest, riot grrrl sprung out of feminist writings and ideas, published often in early handmade zines like *Puncture*, which featured pieces like "Women, Sex and Rock & Roll" and "Women in Rock: An Open Letter." Other important riot grrrl zines included *Interrobang?!* and *Jigsaw*. Musically, influences from early mainstream rock stars like Joan Jett, Janis Joplin, Sonic Youth's Kim Gordon, and others were essential in creating a new reality for women in music. No longer would they be relegated to the sidelines. Women should be in the spotlight and powerfully so, the collective's ethos explained.

Local bands associated with the riot grrrl movement of the 1990s include Bikini Kill (fronted by Kathleen Hanna), Sleater-Kinney, the Gits (though the Ohio-born band didn't always accept this designation), Bratmobile, 7 Year Bitch, Excuse 17, and Heavens to Betsy. But there are many more making up the movement. Adding fuel to the fire, the Olympia-based label, K Records—co-owned by (former intern) Candice Pedersen—was a strong force in spreading the sounds and messages of the riot grrrl ethos. The label worked with a number of the bands and highlighted countless women during its indie music festival, International Pop Underground Convention, which was held at the historic Capitol Theater. Another Olympia label, Kill Rock Stars, is also credited for releasing music from several riot grrrl acts.

But like any movement, riot grrrl wasn't perfect. While the issue of racism was mentioned, riot grrrl in its early stages focused almost exclusively on the voices and issues presented by white women. Central Seattle figures like Tina Bell of Bam Bam were left out of early riot grrrl and grunge conversations, as was IMIJ frontwoman Shannon Funchess. The all-Black band Sista Grrrls is just one example of a project not led by white women exiting the riot grrrl movement, noting at the time that their voices went largely unheard. To wit, the Afropunk community was later created out of the reality of erasure that Black bands felt in the early "progressive" scenes, despite the fact that Black artists helped define early aspects of the punk genre. Today, though, the riot grrrl movement forges ahead on a trajectory that, although still not perfect, has become more inclusive of women of color, transgender women, and nonbinary artists.

SOUNDGARDEN

SINGLE: "BLACK HOLE SUN"

RECORD: SUPERUNKNOWN

RELEASED: 1994 | **RECORDED IN:** SEATTLE

PRODUCER: MICHAEL BEINHORN, SOUNDGARDEN | **LABEL:** A&M RECORDS

When listing the grunge core four—Nirvana, Pearl Jam, Alice in Chains, and Soundgarden—the first three might get the most love. But it was Soundgarden that broke through first, helping to pave the way for the others. Formed in 1984, Soundgarden was first comprised of banshee singer Chris Cornell, lead guitarist Kim Thayil, and bassist Hiro Yamamoto. Originally, Cornell played drums, but the handsome frontman traded the kit for center stage in 1985 when Scott Sundquist joined (replaced a year later by legendary local drummer Matt Cameron). Yamamoto was also replaced, first by Jason Everman and then by Ben Shepherd around 1991. Soundgarden was the first of the big four grunge bands to sign to Sub Pop, recording with Jack Endino and releasing EPs in 1987 and 1988. The band also released its debut LP, *Ultramega OK*, in 1988, earning its first Grammy nomination in 1990.

More albums followed—*Louder Than Love* in 1989, *Badmotorfinger* in 1991, *Superunknown* in 1994, *Down on the Upside* in 1996, and, after a post-turn-of-the-century hiatus, *King Animal* in 2012.

But it was the 1994 LP that made the group immortal, thanks to its iconic song "Black Hole Sun." Written by Cornell, a three-time Grammy Award-winning musician who cofounded Seattle's Temple of the Dog and the L.A. rock band Audioslave, and who tragically died by suicide in 2017, "Black Hole Sun" has come to be known as Soundgarden's signature track, above others like "Fell on Black Days" and "Spoonman." The skyscraping number was the Billboard Modern Rock Tracks No. 1 song for 1994, helping *Superunknown* debut at No. 1 on the Billboard 200.

IMIJ

SINGLE: "MEDGAR EVERS DGC BILL CLINTON AND ME/I"

RECORD: THE IN GODS YOU LUST

RELEASED: 1994 | **RECORDED IN:** SEATTLE

PRODUCER: STEVE FISK | **LABEL:** BABYLON RECORDS

When most think of grunge in Seattle, bands like Nirvana, Pearl Jam, Soundgarden, and Alice in Chains are almost always the go-to. With the national success that these groups enjoyed, it's easy to understand why. But there was another band, not as well-known, that had an impact on the genre just the same: IMIJ.

The members named their band after the famous guitarist and hometown hero, Jimi Hendrix—simply spelling "Jimi" backwards. IMIJ was on the verge of a big record deal, but as happened with many all-Black rock bands in history, labels ultimately passed them over. As recently as the '90s, many labels sadly only thought of Black rock groups as a number to fill a quota, not a place to invest—despite the fact Black Americans invented the musical style!

Though overlooked, IMIJ deserves to be remembered in Seattle history as not only an incredible collective but as a groundbreaking one too. Comprised of Shannon Funchess, Cris Omowale, Lonnie King, Cedric Ross, and Dave "Davee C"

Carpenter, the group's album *The in Gods You Lust* is a thrilling four-song EP that includes a track ("Crackdominium") about the making and selling of drugs at an apartment complex across the street from where band members used to live. The EP also includes the delightfully lewd George Clinton cover, "No Head No Backstage Pass."

But it is the first track on the EP that caught the most attention—"Medgar Evers DGC Bill Clinton and Me/I." Starting with what sounds like nature noises, in drops a quick, tightly tuned snare shot by Carpenter, followed by a giant kick drum *bang*. Guitarist Omowale has said that this song was origin-ally much faster when they first played it, but over time, the band decided to take it down to half the speed, giving it an even heftier feel. This remains one of the best grunge songs from Seattle, period. Though they never got the recognition they deserved, IMIJ should be celebrated and heard. *Very* loudly.

SUNNY DAY REAL ESTATE

SINGLE: "SEVEN"

RECORD: DIARY

RELEASED: 1994 | **RECORDED IN:** CHICAGO

PRODUCER: BRAD WOOD | **LABEL:** SUB POP RECORDS

Sunny Day Real Estate happened at the right time. The group's debut LP, *Diary*, iconic amongst "emo" music fans, was released mere weeks after grunge rocker Kurt Cobain took his own life. With that death, the music landscape across the world, and especially in the Pacific Northwest, changed. A bomb had gone off and people had to recover. Bands like Weezer (which released its *Blue Album* the same day as *Diary*, May 10, 1994) and Sunny Day Real Estate became the soundtrack for that new collective sorrow. Emotive, more melodic bands like Death Cab for Cutie would come on the scene and fill the void closer to the turn of the century, but in 1994, it was Sunny Day Real Estate to the rescue.

Diary is often thought to define the "second wave" of emo, which was first manifested as a genre from music spawned in the Washington, DC, hardcore punk rock scene. The new iteration, though, was characterized by cerebral, unorthodox vocals and jangling electric guitar. Today, *Diary* is one of Sub Pop's

bestselling albums ever, selling more than 230,000 copies, and its opening song, "Seven," showcases lead singer Jeremy Enigk's guttural, wending cries and the band's gripping rhythms. Since its release, the band, which has its roots in the University of Washington campus, has released four studio LPs, and has broken up and gotten back together several times over the years, including for a slot on the 2023 Bumbershoot music festival lineup.

CRITTERS BUGGIN

SINGLE: "SHAG"

RECORD: GUEST

RELEASED: 1994 | **RECORDED IN:** SEATTLE

PRODUCER: DENNIS HERRING, STONE GOSSARD, CRITTERS BUGGIN

LABEL: LOOSEGROOVE

The debut album from the Seattle-based instrumental group Critters Buggin was recorded in Stone Gossard's basement. The Pearl Jam guitarist dug the artists' experimental sound so much that he found time to produce and put it on the record at the height of grunge. He even brought in iconic Seattle grunge singer Shawn Smith to feature on the track "Naked Truth." Critters Buggin, which was comprised of drummer Matt Chamberlain, bassist Brad Houser, vibraphonist Mike Dillon, and saxophonist Skerik, opened minds and ears with each controlled chaotic phrase. Together, they created a sound that could loosely be called jazz, but it also includes industrial, psyche rock, African beats, cosmic vibes, and more.

Each of the artists have played with other significant names in popular music before and since too. Chamberlain with Pearl Jam and Brandi Carlile, Houser with the New Bohemians, and Dillon and Skerik with Les Claypool of

Primus. Skerik also played with the short-lived grunge supergroup Mad Season and with R.E.M. guitarist (and part-time PNW resident) Peter Buck in the instrumental band Tuatara. As Critters Buggin, the quartet released seven albums and two EPs from 1994 to 2014, a handful of which came out on Gossard's Loosegroove record label. The 9-track LP *Guest*—the band's first—is rich with immersive compositions, ranging from just over a minute to nearly thirteen. It's a significant work, not only as an album but as a flash point for the careers of four elite players.

THE PRESIDENTS OF THE UNITED STATES OF AMERICA

SINGLE: "PEACHES"

RECORD: THE PRESIDENTS OF THE UNITED STATES OF AMERICA

RELEASED: 1995 | **RECORDED IN:** SEATTLE

PRODUCER: CONRAD UNO, CHRIS BALLEW, DAVE DEDERER

LABEL: POPLLAMA, COLUMBIA

Winner for the longest band name in Seattle history, the Presidents of the United States of America were seemingly ubiquitous when it came to mainstream rock radio in the mid-1990s, thanks to charming songs like "Peaches." The group, which formed in Seattle in 1993, was comprised of singer Chris Ballew, drummer Jason Finn, and guitarist Dave Dederer. The band's debut self-titled album, released in 1995, went triple platinum.

Later, Ballew, burnt out on the industry, went solo, eventually finding a successful career in writing and releasing kids music under the moniker Caspar Babypants. But before all that went down, the group was on top of the main-stream music world. Their debut LP included hits like the cartoonish "Lump" and "Kitty." But it was "Peaches," which hit No. 8 on the Billboard

Modern Rock Tracks, that made them globally beloved. The track, which earned the band a Grammy nomination, was born out of an odd day. Ballew was waiting at a bus stop one afternoon when a "disheveled man in an oily overcoat with a big beard" came walking by, saying over and over, "I'm moving to the country, gonna eat a lot of peaches." He filed the line away and it soon landed in the group's best-known song.

Ballew has since said the success of the song brought both validation and chaos, financial reward and (too much) touring. It also gave the band a chance to meet former president Bill Clinton and the pop star Madonna, who courted the group to her music label.

CLINTON FEARON

SINGLE: "NAH FORGET MI ROOTS"

RECORD: DISTURB THE DEVIL

RELEASED: 1995 | **RECORDED IN:** SEATTLE

PRODUCER: CLINTON FEARON | **LABEL:** BOOGIE BROWN RECORDS

Reggae star Clinton Fearon moved to Seattle in 1987 and, ever since, he's been making music beloved around the globe. Often seen with his acoustic guitar, singing songs at summer festivals and doling out melodic words of wisdom to fans of all ages while wearing his trademark cap, Fearon was born on January 13, 1951, near Kingston, Jamaica.

He was first inspired to make music through his church. As a young adult in 1969, he was playing with his group the Brothers when he was recruited to join the nationally popular Jamaican roots reggae band the Gladiators. Fearon starred as a singer and musician in the big-name trio, which released dozens of albums and recorded hits like "Mix Up" and "Hearsay," until the time he decided to relocate to Seattle and begin his solo career.

In the Northwest, Fearon launched his project the Boogie Brown Band, which included the 1994 debut LP *Disturb the Devil*. Since,

Fearon has dropped more than a dozen albums, including *Breaking News*, in 2022. To open his debut solo LP, Clinton made a statement. While he was going solo with his own project in a new country, he noted that he'd never forget his roots or where he came from. But that's not the sole message the opening track makes. Fearon also sings about historical divides and sources of great pain, from Jesus and Judas to war and slavery. In this way, we all have to remember the past. Good and bad. It's a bold thought, necessary as ever, delivered with a chunking reggae guitar and Fearon's bubbly, hopeful voice.

7 YEAR BITCH

SINGLE: "24,900 MILES PER HOUR"

RECORD: GATO NEGRO

RELEASED: 1996 | **RECORDED IN:** SAN FRANCISCO

PRODUCER: BILLY ANDERSON, 7 YEAR BITCH | **LABEL:** ATLANTIC RECORDS

Named after the term *seven-year itch*, this seminal Seattle-born punk rock band rose to prominence in unison with the burgeoning riot grrrl movement of the 1990s. Though its career was marked by tragedy, the group's impact was large.

Formed by vocalist Selene Vigil, guitarist Stefanie Sargent, drummer Valerie Agnew, and bassist Elizabeth Davis, the band began playing shows in 1990, and after its first gig, they opened for the influential Ohio-born punk group, the Gits. 7 Year Bitch released its debut LP *Sick 'Em* in October 1992. But Sargent's untimely, drug-induced death months prior put a pall over the achievement. A year later, the band's close friend and Gits frontwoman, Mia Zapata, was murdered in Seattle, sending more shock waves throughout the band and its community.

Yet, the band members pressed on. Agnew later became a central figure in the Seattle-based anti-violence and self-defense group Home Alive. In 1995, 7 Year Bitch signed with Atlantic Records, and they released their third and final studio LP, the 12-song *Gato Negro*, in 1996. (The band would also release a live album, *Live at Moe*, in 2016.) The album included three singles, including "24,900 Miles Per Hour," an unabashed crash of a song that showcases Vigil's compelling, melodic, and vengeful voice. Other singles from the LP include "Miss Understood" and "The History of My Future." In a perhaps ironic twist of fate, 7 Year Bitch broke up in 1997, seven years after it started. Yet, their legacy remains intact, the band a beacon of perseverance and progressiveness for others that followed.

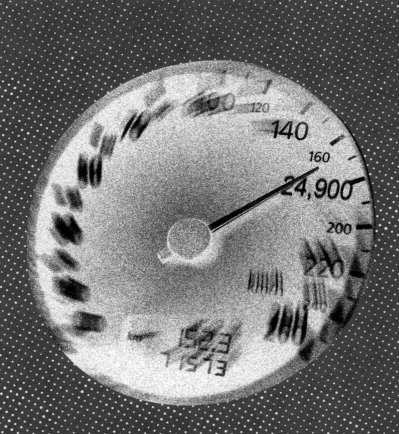

VITAMIN D (GHETTO CHILDREN)

SINGLE: "WHO'S LISTENING"

RECORD: DO THE MATH

RELEASED: 1996 | **RECORDED IN:** SEATTLE

PRODUCER: VITAMIN D | **LABEL:** TRIBAL MUSIC INC.

Any conversation about the "sound of Seattle" cannot be complete without honoring and acknowledging the work of one of the city's formative hip-hop legends, Derrick "Vitamin D" Brown. The artist, who grew up in a musical family, has long been a crucial influence on the PNW. With guitarist Herman Brown—a session musician with Motown Records—for a father and jazz-playing Clarence Oliphant for a maternal grandfather, it's no wonder that a funk and soul influence seeped into Vitamin D's unique and innovative production style. His musical family doesn't stop there. Brown's cousin Eddie Wells, also known as "Sugar Bear," was a member of Seattle's trailblazing hip-hop group the Emerald Street Boys. In fact, he gave Vitamin D his first set of turntables, but it wasn't until the late 1980s when

Vitamin D began to seriously pursue music as a profession.

Respected for his solo work, the beat-maker is also known for groups like Ghetto Children (with rapper B Self) and Source of Labor, in which he partnered with local hip-hop ambassador and educator Jonathan Moore (a.k.a. Wordsayer). Indeed, Moore is credited with bringing Seattle hip-hop into the mainstream in many ways, both as a performer and show producer. Vitamin D is also a visionary, mentoring many (including prolific producer Jake One) and credited with creating Tribal Music Inc., an influential hip-hop label that released compilations of various Seattle hip-hop acts, primarily produced and engineered by Vitamin D in his now-iconic home studio, the Pharmacy. Since then, he has worked with acts like Kendrick Lamar, 50 Cent, Redman, and Macklemore. He even gets a shoutout in Mack's 2013 song "The Town." Without a doubt Vitamin D's contributions are fundamental to the conversation of the Seattle sound. In a town that's usually overcast, everyone could use a little more Vitamin D in their lives.

SLEATER-KINNEY

SINGLE: "DIG ME OUT"

RECORD: DIG ME OUT

RELEASED: 1997 | **RECORDED IN:** SEATTLE

PRODUCER: JOHN GOODMANSON | **LABEL:** KILL ROCK STARS

In a way, Sleater-Kinney has only risen in popularity since the band's debut in 1994. The punk rock group, fronted by musician Corin Tucker and musician-actor-writer-comedian Carrie Brownstein (the co-creator of the popular sketch comedy series *Portlandia*), has enjoyed some increased attention of late thanks to Brownstein's heightened visibility. (Rumor has it that Brownstein is also writing a biopic about the rock band Heart.)

Even without the *Portlandia* bump, the group would be central to the history of the region's music. The band formed in Olympia in the mid-1990s, naming itself after a road near Lacey, Washington outside of Olympia. Founded by Brownstein and Tucker, Sleater-Kinney welcomed standout drummer Janet Weiss. She left the group in 2019, making her Sleater-Kinney's longest-running third member. The group emerged as part of the influential riot grrrl movement—Tucker had previously been in the band Heavens to Betsy, while Brownstein played in the group Excuse 17.

The pair recorded their first album while on a trip in Australia, staying up on the final night to record the songs for their self-titled release. While Sleater-Kinney boasts eleven LPs to date, including 2024's *Little Rope*, it was their 1997 album, *Dig Me Out*, that first included Weiss on the kit. Earlier this decade, *Rolling Stone* ranked *Dig Me Out* as No. 189 of the 500 greatest albums of all time. The band released two singles from the album, but it was a third track, the LP's title song, that made the biggest waves at home, becoming one of the most popular songs that year on legendary Seattle radio station KEXP. On the title track, Tucker's vocals soar over buzzy guitar and drums—a laser beam cutting through smoke.

PIGEONHED

SINGLE: "BATTLE FLAG"

RECORD: THE FULL SENTENCE

RELEASED: 1997 | **RECORDED IN:** SEATTLE

PRODUCER: JOHN GOODMANSON, PIGEONHED | **LABEL:** SUB POP RECORDS

The funk rock project of producer Steve Fisk and songwriter and vocalist Shawn Smith, Pigeonhed started in 1993 and stopped in 1997. In its final year, though, the band released the sophomore album *The Full Sentence*, which included the electronic, brash track "Battle Flag." Smith, who passed away in 2019 at age fifty-three, bounces on the song, channeling Prince. The beat slaps with a fat bassline and funky ambiance. Later, it was remixed by the British group Lo Fidelity Allstars on the album *Flash Bulb Emergency Overflow Cavalcade of Remixes*, and eventually it gained traction and attention, hitting No. 36 on the UK Singles Chart and No. 6 on Billboard Modern Rock Tracks. It was also used in the NBC hit show *ER*. The Lo Fidelity Allstars version hits a bit harder, with bigger, sharper, more emphatic drums. It's transformed while also honoring the source material.

Pigeonhed reunited in 2010 and remained together until Smith's passing. The singer was beloved, and many in the city mourned his death. Smith sang with Pearl Jam's Mike McCready in the group

Flight to Mars and was also the frontman for the popular grunge group Brad. That band, formed in 1992, featured Pearl Jam guitarist Stone Gossard and Regan Hagar of Andrew Wood's Malfunkshun among its lineup and went on to release a new album with Smith's last recordings in 2023. After Smith died, Seattle guitarist Kathy Moore wrote a brilliant ode to the Spokane-born singer. "Someday We'll Fly," from the Kathy Moore Super Power Trio album *I Won't Let the End of the World Bring Me Down*, features a weeping, heavens-shattering solo befitting of the remarkable musical figure.

FOO FIGHTERS

SINGLE: "EVERLONG"

RECORD: THE COLOUR AND THE SHAPE

RELEASED: 1997 | **RECORDED IN:** WOODINVILLE, WA; LOS ANGELES; WASHINGTON, DC

PRODUCER: GIL NORTON | **LABEL:** ROSWELL, CAPITOL

It was March 18, 1998, when Dave Grohl went on the Howard Stern radio show and changed his life. Grohl, of course, had been the drummer for the iconic grunge band Nirvana, which dissolved after the death of frontman Kurt Cobain in 1994. A year later, Grohl released the debut self-titled Foo Fighters album, recorded at Robert Lang Studios in Seattle. On it, he played all the instruments. But it was the band's second album, *The Colour and the Shape*, released in 1997, that really put Grohl on the map, thanks to singles like "My Hero" and "Everlong." On Stern's radio show in March of 1998, Grohl played the rhythmically thick "Everlong" acoustic for the first time. And that's when the world knew he was a true frontman.

Everlong also happens to be the last song ever performed in public by Foo Fighters drummer, the late Taylor Hawkins, who died in March of 2022 while the band was on tour in South America. "Everlong" was written in drop D tuning while Grohl was living at a friend's house in Virginia,

sleeping in a sleeping bag while going through
a divorce. He says the track is about "a girl
that I'd fallen in love with" (artist Louise Post
from the Chicago-born band Veruca Salt). When it
was released in 1997, *The Colour and the Shape*
spawned three singles in the top 10 on US rock
radio charts, and the album hit No. 10 on the
Billboard 200.

Foo Fighters, originally comprised of Grohl, Nate
Mendel on bass, and William Goldsmith on drums
(both formerly of Sunny Day Real Estate), along
with guitarist Pat Smear, who had toured with
Nirvana, has gone through a few lineup changes in
its history. Early on, Goldsmith and Smear left
and Grohl brought on Chris Shiflett to play guitar
and Hawkins to play drums. But Smear came back in
2005 and keyboardist Rami Jaffee joined in 2017.
Now, the band has a new drummer, Josh Freese, to
replace Hawkins. To date, Foo Fighters have won
fifteen Grammy Awards and have a well-deserved
place in rock history.

HARVEY DANGER

SINGLE: "FLAGPOLE SITTA"

RECORD: WHERE HAVE ALL THE MERRYMAKERS GONE?

RELEASED: 1997 | **RECORDED IN:** SEATTLE

PRODUCER: JOHN GOODMANSON, HARVEY DANGER | **LABEL:** ARENA ROCK

In the terrific 2015 music documentary *The Glamour & the Squalor* about iconic Seattle radio DJ Marco Collins, the former KNDD disc-jockey tells the story of singer Sean Nelson approaching him one night outside the station. Nelson, the frontman for the local band Harvey Danger, gave Collins a copy of their new debut LP, *Where Have All the Merrymakers Gone?* The album was performing well on college radio, but it hadn't quite broken the band commercially and, as such, the group was considering disbanding. But after Collins got his hand on the album, the record's hit track, "Flagpole Sitta," became the influential station's most requested song in early 1998.

The story highlights the power of Collins, the radio, and, most importantly, Harvey Danger. Yes, "Flagpole Sitta" was a huge success across the United States. The song hit No. 38 on the Billboard Hot 100 Airplay chart and it was a fixture on MTV. It features Nelson's thoughtful, weird, and poetic lyrics. Nelson, who would later write for the local paper *The Stranger*, has remained a central presence in Seattle arts for years, even acting in a Lynn Shelton film, *My Effortless Brilliance*. Harvey Danger, which formed in 1992, was originally comprised of Nelson, the late bassist Aaron Huffman, Jeff J. Lin on guitar, and drummer Evan Sult. During the band's career, the group released three LPs from 1997 to 2005. But the band never quite regained the popularity that "Flagpole Sitta" carved out.

MAKTUB

SINGLE: "LOVE ME LIKE BEFORE"

RECORD: SUBTLE WAYS

RELEASED: 1999 | **RECORDED IN:** SEATTLE

PRODUCER: BRAD SMITH | **LABEL:** JASIRI MEDIA GROUP

Fans of late-night television know the name Reggie Watts. He was the leader of the house band for *The Late Late Show with James Corden*, providing unusual sounds, songs, accompaniment, and ideas to the talk show format. Before that, however, Watts was offering similar music to audiences in Seattle. Born in West Germany on March 23, 1972, Watts moved around a lot with his family during his youth. At eighteen, though, he landed in the Emerald City, studying at the Art Institute of Seattle and later the acclaimed Cornish College of the Arts.

In 1996, Watts formed the band Maktub (an Arabic word that means "destiny") with Davis Martin, Kevin Goldman, and Alex Veley. The band released its debut album, *Subtle Ways*, in 1999, followed by *Khronos* in 2003 and three more records after that. Their best-known song is likely the soul-rock track "Just Like Murder," a combination of Lenny Kravitz and Ben Harper, showcasing Watts's malleable and memorable singing voice. "Love Me Like Before," from the band's debut, is more sonically subdued. Listening to it now, you can hear the beginnings of the band's sound that would develop and soar on future tracks and albums. Maktub added guitar player Thaddeus Turner in 2000 to bolster its sound.

Watts—a singer, songwriter, piano player, and multi-instrumentalist inspired to play music after seeing the one-time Seattle resident Ray Charles, and who later toured as a keys player for Wayne Horvitz—moved from Seattle in the early 2000s to pursue his career in New York City. A comedian, he's also released standup specials, such as *Reggie Watts: Spatial* on Netflix, and a handful of solo albums. What he'll do post–*Late Late Show* is anyone's guess.

The 2000s

BEN GIBBARD ON
GETTING PAST TRAGEDY IN THE AUGHTS

When Death Cab for Cutie's Ben Gibbard looks back on the post-grunge era in Seattle, he doesn't immediately think of his own band—he thinks of Modest Mouse. For Gibbard, whose Bellingham-born group would earn platinum album status and Grammy nominations after releasing their debut LP, *Something About Airplanes*, it is Modest Mouse, fronted by creative dynamo Isaac Brock, that kicked off the new sound in the area. As Seattle was quickly becoming culturally "uncool" again post-grunge, there was a growing sense of distance between the city and the rest of the world. And Brock's songs highlighted it accurately, aided by the band's own geographic distance from Seattle.

Modest Mouse formed in Issaquah, Washington, a historically rural suburb some twenty miles from the city. After releasing several records, the band finally broke onto the national scene with its 2004 single, "Float On." The group's guitar-based tracks are rooted in rock, but lyrically steered away from much of what was popular in the early '90s. In some ways, the music returned the focus back to the fringe sensibilities of the Northwest. By then, the balloon had popped from the grunge gold rush, but there stood Modest Mouse, along with other bands like Boise's Built to Spill, carrying on the irreverent, askew perspective that has been signature to the Upper Left.

"In the early aughts, it was not cool to be from Seattle," Gibbard says. "In 2001 it was the White Stripes, Interpol, the Strokes, Yeah Yeah Yeahs. What was cool had shifted far away from here."

But in a way, Seattle has always excelled when it didn't concern itself with being cool. The area was returning to what it knew best: *modesty*. For Gibbard, the best part of the city's music culture is the humility it breeds among its participants. After all, what good is a popped balloon? He's proud to be from the area and wouldn't want to be from anywhere else, he says, because the community keeps its artists grounded—it's practically imprinted. Everyone here's a misfit at the end of the American highways, so why pretend otherwise?

"I think there's something that's been instilled in us from our heroes in the '90s on," Gibbard says. "You can get famous outside of Seattle, you can become successful. But at the end of the day, you have to treat people and the scene with respect. And not carry yourself like you are above it or better than it or didn't come from it."

Like Modest Mouse, Death Cab for Cutie rose to prominence at an inflection point in the city's music history. The '90s brought eyes and ears galore to the area, and the music industry—due to CD sales and candy-coated pop groups— was "flush with cash," Gibbard says. Bands were getting million-dollar deals and doing nothing with them, leading to a lot of sunk costs, which the industry could absorb. Until it couldn't, and the executives and scouts and A & R people began to leave. Suddenly the city was largely on its own again. No more people "sniffing around" for new talent. But the region soldiered on.

Influential radio host Marco Collins and radio station KNDD were crucial to the continually developing music scene, as were local venues. Gibbard remembers playing on three-band bills at places like the Crocodile Cafe and Sit & Spin. At the time, before the industry frenzy abated, there were still bands hoping to be plucked from oblivion and put on a tour bus headed toward fame and fortune, he says. But then it just all went away. (This period coincided with the rise of computer file sharing, Napster, and LimeWire.) The music industry was changing rapidly, both locally and globally. A few bands, including Death Cab, were able to navigate the shift and make it through.

Gibbard remembers playing the Fairhaven Auditorium in Bellingham in January 1999. Local luminaries like Damien Jurado and Pedro the Lion were on the bill. A fresh hope was blooming. There were some three hundred people and Gibbard remembers looking around and thinking: *This is working*. He kept seeing strangers at shows. Audiences grew. He remembers an earlier gig, the CD release party for *Something About Airplanes* in 1998 at the Crocodile Cafe in the Belltown neighborhood of Seattle. The Minus 5 (with R.E.M.'s Peter Buck), Peter Parker, and Western State Hurricanes were on the bill, and three hundred people were in the audience.

"I came offstage, and I broke down in tears," Gibbard says. "I realized in that moment, *this is real*. Not that I would ever have foreseen the career that we had. But I had that realization, *this is working*. This is a real band."

Now, a few decades later, Gibbard is doing that for other

groups, bringing local artists like the Black Tones and Chong the Nomad up for opening slots at big shows at the Showbox or the Paramount Theatre, giving them a chance to shed a tear and experience the crowd's love. As an up-and-coming musician in the '90s, Gibbard knew what it was like to see icons on TV and feel that they were far away, untouchable. Maybe that's why the local stars have always tried to make sure to eschew that distance when they're home. Just as genres like punk and indie rock are welcoming to all types of players, Seattle's

best can be too. From Heart to Pearl Jam to Sir Mix-a-Lot to Modest Mouse to Death Cab and beyond, those who call Seattle home are family.

Gibbard sums it up nicely: "The idea that you would get famous outside of Seattle and then be showing up at a bar or a club trying to get in for free, saying, 'Yeah but I'm famous!' is the kind of thing we laugh about people trying to do here!"

Sounds about right.

▲ The Crocodile Cafe in its original location, Seattle, 2005

PEDRO THE LION

SINGLE: "OPTIONS"

RECORD: CONTROL

RELEASED: 2002 | **RECORDED IN:** SEATTLE

PRODUCER: DAVID BAZAN | **LABEL:** JADE TREE

Known for living room performance tours, a cult following, and indie community respect, David Bazan is a songwriter's songwriter. His most well-known project is Pedro the Lion, the band he formed in the mid-1990s. A "son of Evangelical Christianity," Bazan has battled with religious concepts for much of his adult life, something he talks about in the acclaimed documentary *Strange Negotiations*. He was once considered a crossover Christian artist but no longer identifies with the faith. Still, he remains a powerful artist, as much a poet as a performer, part Randy Newman, part Kurt Cobain.

In 1997, Pedro the Lion released its debut EP, *Whole*. But the band's third album, *Control* (2002), garnered significant attention with its themes of capitalism, marriage, and death. The concept was influenced by the 1999 World Trade Organization protests in Seattle, telling the story of a businessman killed by his wife after having an affair. It's been called the *OK Computer* for the Christian coffee shop community

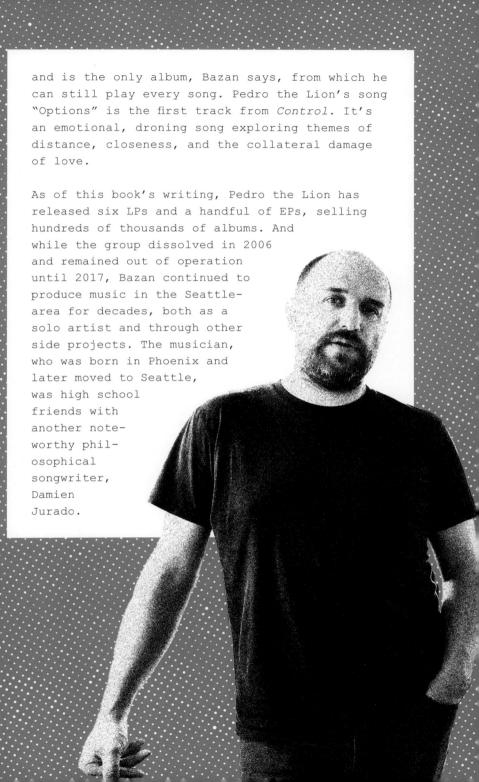

and is the only album, Bazan says, from which he can still play every song. Pedro the Lion's song "Options" is the first track from *Control*. It's an emotional, droning song exploring themes of distance, closeness, and the collateral damage of love.

As of this book's writing, Pedro the Lion has released six LPs and a handful of EPs, selling hundreds of thousands of albums. And while the group dissolved in 2006 and remained out of operation until 2017, Bazan continued to produce music in the Seattle-area for decades, both as a solo artist and through other side projects. The musician, who was born in Phoenix and later moved to Seattle, was high school friends with another note-worthy phil-osophical songwriter, Damien Jurado.

THE POSTAL SERVICE

SINGLE: "SUCH GREAT HEIGHTS"

RECORD: GIVE UP

RELEASED: 2003 | **RECORDED IN:** SEATTLE, LOS ANGELES

PRODUCER: THE POSTAL SERVICE | **LABEL:** SUB POP RECORDS

Although this electronic supergroup only released one album during their time together, it was all they needed to make a sonic impact on American music. To wit, the record *Give Up* was certified RIAA platinum and charted at No. 45 on the Billboard 200.

The group began in 2001 and released its sole album two years later on Sub Pop. It quickly became the label's second-most successful release, after Nirvana's *Bleach*. Band members include Ben Gibbard (Death Cab for Cutie), Jenny Lewis (Rilo Kiley), and producer Jimmy Tamborello (a.k.a. Dntel). In the beginning, Gibbard and Tamborello began sending demos back and forth via the United States Postal Service, which served as the inspiration for their name. Unfortunately, not long after the group gained some success, the actual USPS did not show love for the use of their name and sent the band a cease-and-desist letter in 2003. Thankfully, the two came to an agreement, which led to collaborations between the parties, including a performance promoting the actual

Postal Service. The USPS even sold the group's album on its website.

The Seattle-born trio stayed active until 2005. Then in 2013, after an eight-year hiatus, the Postal Service reunited to celebrate the ten-year anniversary of its debut album with a tour and reissue. Other contributions on the original LP came from artists like Jen Wood (of the group Tattle Tale), who is heard singing backup vocals on the recording of the song "Such Great Heights." Wood also joined the band on tour for a few shows. Grunge drum legend Barrett Martin has joined the Postal Service on tour too.

In 2022, the band announced a co-headlining tour with Gibbard's other band, Death Cab for Cutie. Both groups were celebrating twenty-year anniver-saries. For the electronic group it was for *Give Up* and for the indie rock group it was for their impactful LP *Transatlanticism*. While the Postal Service has just the one release to its name, the LP was a collection of tracks that made its mark, with songs appearing in commercials, movies, and television shows. And "Such Great Heights" is four minutes of beautiful, crafted melodies that make you—and its creators, we can only imag-ine—feel like swimming in a lucid dream.

THE
MUSEUM
OF POP
CULTURE

325 5TH AVENUE N, SEATTLE

In Seattle, the legend of late Microsoft cofounder Paul Allen lives on, in large part through music. The tech giant, who passed away in 2018, was a well-known guitar player in his spare time. He even hired musicians to tour the globe via his yacht, landing at film festivals. He also founded the short-lived Upstream music festival in Seattle in 2017. But another way Allen's spirit and affection for songs live on is through the Museum of Pop Culture (nicknamed MoPop). The facility is an homage to music, Seattle's own personal Rock & Roll Hall of Fame.

The museum, which Allen founded in 2000, is built in the shadow of the Space Needle and was first called the Experience Music Project (renamed in 2016). Dozens of prominent musical exhibits have showcased artists like Pearl Jam and Jimi Hendrix. The museum also sponsors annual pop music conferences and twenty-one-and-under battles of the bands known as Sound Off! It's home to many sci-fi exhibits and popular film festivals too.

The Museum of Pop Culture's exterior is unlike any building in Seattle. Designed by renowned architect and designer Frank Gehry, the structures resemble large upside-down buckets of bent, multicolored sheet metal. Gehry has designed other prominent buildings in this fashion, including the Walt Disney Concert Hall. Not everyone loves the design—*Forbes* magazine called it one of the world's ten ugliest buildings.

In total, MoPop is 140,000 square feet and features the Sky Church, named in honor of Jimi Hendrix, which can hold up to eight hundred in the audience. It often hosts regular music events, from concerts with big names to celebrations for the local Grammy chapter. The museum also holds its regular Founders Awards for artists whose "noteworthy contributions continued to nurture the next generation of risk-takers." The first recipients were the sisters of Heart, Ann and Nancy Wilson. Others have included Brandi Carlile, Alice in Chains, and Quincy Jones. At its core, the venue celebrates music, art, and culture, especially of the local variety, and visitors return over and over again to experience Seattle through MoPop's unique lens.

THE BLOOD BROTHERS

SINGLE: "LIVE AT THE APOCALYPSE CABARET"

RECORD: CRIMES

RELEASED: 2004 | **RECORDED IN:** SEATTLE

PRODUCER: JOHN GOODMANSON | **LABEL:** V2

Like a snake with two heads, the PNW post-hard-core group the Blood Brothers could hypnotize and strike from any direction. Singers Johnny Whitney and Jordan Billie founded the band, which released its debut album, *This Adultery Is Ripe*, in 2000. The record thrashes with screams and rampaging choruses. In one moment, Whitney and Billie are performing in unison, in another they've deviated into their own coils of vocal attack. The band's central lineup included drummer Mark Gajadhar, along with bassist Morgan Henderson and guitarist Cody Votolato (who replaced original six-string player Devin Welch). Together, they released five EPs and five LPs from 2000 to 2006, with the final two albums charting on the Billboard 200. The group disbanded in 2007, but Epitaph Records re-released much of its catalog in 2009.

The Blood Brothers' 2004 LP *Crimes* marked an evolution for the group. It was the band's first major label release, and both vocalists boasted a refinement to their singing. Still brash and bold, still shrieking, their skills had been honed and their lyrical fangs sharpened. The album itself is largely a commentary on President Bush's time in office, from jabs at the news media to direct hits on the US military industrial complex. The record, produced in Seattle's historic Robert Lang Studios, is much like a Jackson Pollock painting—hectic and hypnotizing. After the group split, its members went on to participate in other projects around the city and beyond, from Champagne Champagne to the Fleet Foxes and Yeah Yeah Yeahs. The Blood Brothers reunited briefly in 2014 for a few live shows and perhaps, if we're lucky, they might get the band back together to again offer the band's signature bite.

MODEST MOUSE

SINGLE: "FLOAT ON"

RECORD: GOOD NEWS FOR PEOPLE WHO LOVE BAD NEWS

RELEASED: 2004 | **RECORDED IN:** OXFORD, MS; MEMPHIS, TN

PRODUCER: DENNIS HERRING | **LABEL:** EPIC

The hit song "Float On" by the Issaquah-born rock band Modest Mouse feels like a burst of serotonin. It's one thousand "likes" on your latest social media post. It's addictive. It's bright, flashy, and sticky like watermelon bubble gum. From lead singer Isaac Brock's pleasantly rough, Velcro-like voice to the dancing electric guitar to the bouncy rhythms from bassist Eric Judy, drummer Benjamin Weikel, and multi-instrumentalist Dann Gallucci, it's a shot to the bloodstream.

From the 2004 album, *Good News for People Who Love Bad News*, the album that helped the group achieve mainstream success, "Float On" garnered Modest Mouse a Grammy nomination for Best Rock Song. Brock wrote it intentionally positive, saying it was a "complete conscious thing" to go the upbeat route, given the bleak outlook on climate and the political landscape at the turn of the millennium. Indeed, the song begins with the serendipitous line "I backed my car into a cop car the other day / Well, he just drove off sometimes life's okay." The band's 2004 album, the only

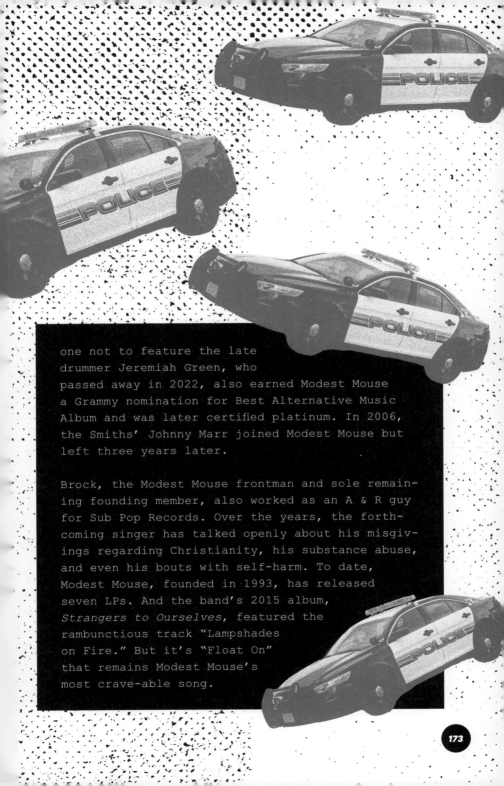

one not to feature the late
drummer Jeremiah Green, who
passed away in 2022, also earned Modest Mouse
a Grammy nomination for Best Alternative Music
Album and was later certified platinum. In 2006,
the Smiths' Johnny Marr joined Modest Mouse but
left three years later.

Brock, the Modest Mouse frontman and sole remaining founding member, also worked as an A & R guy
for Sub Pop Records. Over the years, the forthcoming singer has talked openly about his misgiv-
ings regarding Christianity, his substance abuse,
and even his bouts with self-harm. To date,
Modest Mouse, founded in 1993, has released
seven LPs. And the band's 2015 album,
Strangers to Ourselves, featured the
rambunctious track "Lampshades
on Fire." But it's "Float On"
that remains Modest Mouse's
most crave-able song.

DEATH CAB FOR CUTIE

SINGLE: "I WILL FOLLOW YOU INTO THE DARK"

RECORD: PLANS

RELEASED: 2005 | **RECORDED IN:** NORTH BROOKFIELD, MA

PRODUCER: CHRIS WALLA | **LABEL:** ATLANTIC RECORDS, BARSUK

Death Cab for Cutie might be the most important Seattle-area band to arrive after the mid-1990s grunge movement. For all of its reflective, even at times forlorn mood, the band's success in a new, less-aggressive musical direction offered hope to a new generation of artists. Death Cab making it meant there was light at the end of the tunnel after a time when so many of the city's musical heroes had died too young.

Death Cab, which was born an hour or two north of Seattle in Bellingham, is known for its poetic, intellectual frontman, Ben Gibbard. His sound first earned attention with Death Cab's 1998 debut LP, *Something About Airplanes*. Over the years, the band released nine more albums, including *Asphalt Meadows* in 2022. In 2005, Death Cab released its fifth studio album, the Grammy-nominated *Plans*, which included the heartfelt acoustic offering "I Will Follow You into the Dark." That track, used in television shows and movies galore, is about finding your way through the confusion, even about navigating death. One of the chorus's iconic lines showcases this uncertainy: "If heaven and hell decide that they both are satisfied / Illuminate the noes on their vacancy signs . . ." before concluding with the repeated "Then I'll follow you into the dark." It displays Gibbard's tender, intricate style as well as the universality of his clear-eyed delivery.

Formed in 1997, Death Cab was a solo endeavor at first for Gibbard, but it developed quickly into a full-band project and a platinum-selling, Grammy-nominated rocket ship. But the songwriter didn't stop there. Gibbard is also the cofounder of the platinum-selling electronic group the Postal Service, with producer Jimmy Tamborello and singer Jenny Lewis. With worlds colliding, the two bands linked for a co-headlining tour in 2023.

BAND OF HORSES

SINGLE: "THE FUNERAL"

RECORD: EVERYTHING ALL THE TIME

RELEASED: 2006 | **RECORDED IN:** SEATTLE

PRODUCER: BAND OF HORSES, PHIL EK | **LABEL:** SUB POP RECORDS

When Band of Horses frontman Ben Bridwell landed in Seattle after traveling the country, he was homeless. Bridwell lived on the streets with a sleeping bag tied to his back. Before his eventual Grammy-nominated group, his foray into music began even further back with popular indie rock band Carissa's Wierd.

That group, founded in 1995 in Tucson, Arizona, included accomplished players Matt Brooke, Jenn Champion, and Sera Cahoone. Before it officially broke up, however, Bridwell moved to Seattle with a few of its members and started a new group. That project, Band of Horses, later released its 2006 debut LP, *Everything All the Time*, and Bridwell earned his first Grammy nomination in 2010.

Upon first moving to Seattle, Bridwell got a job with the local Crocodile Cafe. Today, he thanks the venue for hiring him off the street, sleeping bag on his back and all. As he got his feet underneath him, Bridwell connected with Sub Pop Records through its interest in Carissa's Wierd. Around the same time, Bridwell's brother had a friend, Sam Beam, who would send Bridwell music, hoping to land on Bridwell's upstart label, Brown Records. But Bridwell shared the music with Sub Pop, and that's how the label signed Beam's Iron & Wine, a group Band of Horses would later tour with.

Band of Horses recorded its first album with some of the musicians from Carissa's Wierd, but the band has since gone through many lineup changes with Bridwell remaining the lone consistent member. To date, the group has released six studio albums, including the 2006 debut *Everything All the Time* and the most recent *Things Are Great* in 2022. In 2007, the group also released the song, "Detlef Schrempf," an ode to the former member of the Seattle SuperSonics. But it's "The Funeral" from the debut LP that has shown the longest legs. The electric guitar-driven number features Bridwell's swelling, falsetto vocals, dreamy and piercing. He is a ghost, and his sonic haunt is quite lovely.

NEKO CASE

SINGLE: "HOLD ON HOLD ON"

RECORD: FOX CONFESSOR BRINGS THE FLOOD

RELEASED: 2006 | **RECORDED IN:** TUCSON, AZ

PRODUCER: NEKO CASE, DARRYL NEUDORF | **LABEL:** ANTI-

When those familiar with Neko Case think of the artist, her booming, echoing, Liberty Bell–like voice (and maybe also her ocean of red hair) first springs to mind. Case, who was born in Virginia, today considers Tacoma home. The artist attended art school in Vancouver, BC, in the mid-1990s and soon fell in love with the DIY music scene and punk ethic of the Northwest. In Canada, she recorded with then-up-and-coming band the New Pornographers, which have since become an influential group in indie rock.

But Case is best known as a solo artist with a dark, country sound she first developed in Seattle. In 1997, she released her debut LP *The Virginian* with her band the Boyfriends while living in the city. And she released *Furnace Room Lullaby* in 2000 while still living in the Northwest. Her third album, *Blacklisted*, was recorded in Tucson in 2002, as was the 2006 LP, *Fox Confessor Brings the Flood*. Those albums feature Case's perhaps best-known songs, "Deep Red Bells" and "Hold On Hold On," respectively. But

it's the autobiographical "Hold On Hold On" that
shows fans what Case is all about. It's about
the false promise of hope, about isolation and
embracing confused, even dark, feelings, if for
just a few hours. It's about leaving the party
for your quiet room, sung as only Case, a neon
church bell of a singer, can. Case has released
seven studio albums to date (and—fun fact—works
with Rachel Flotard of Visqueen today) and is
a truly original artist in the Pacific Northwest
pastiche of musical history.

KIMYA DAWSON

SINGLE: "LOOSE LIPS"

RECORD: REMEMBER THAT I LOVE YOU

RELEASED: 2006 | **RECORDED IN:** PORTLAND, OR; NEW YORK CITY

PRODUCER: ARION SALAZAR, KIMYA DAWSON | **LABEL:** K RECORDS

Kimya Dawson sings a bit like you might expect a colorful crayon drawing to sing if it could. The Bedford Hills, New York–born artist rose to popularity in 2001 with their duo the Moldy Peaches (with Adam Green). The band's song "Anyone Else but You" earned a prominent spot in the popular, Oscar-nominated 2007 film *Juno*. Known for their stripped-down, playful music, Dawson has even released kids' music, like the album *Alphabutt*. They collaborated with beloved indie rapper Aesop Rock in the project the Uncluded, and they have worked with many big-name artists over the years, including Ben Kweller, They Might Be Giants, the Mountain Goats, and Regina Spektor.

Today, Dawson lives in Washington state and recently released a new collection of songs by the Moldy Peaches with Green. But more than any project, song, or album, Dawson is known for their beautiful, inventive, and even childlike musicianship. That DNA

can be heard clearly in the song "Loose
Lips," from the 2006 album *Remember That
I Love You*. With memorable lines like "My
war paint is Sharpie ink and I'll show you
how much my shit stinks" and the repeated
"Remember that I love you," the song (which
also appeared on the *Juno* soundtrack) calls
for vulnerability, authenticity, and uncon-
ditional love. Dawson, who has released
three albums with the Moldy Peaches along
with eight solo albums and a number of
other releases, remains an essential presence on the local scene.

BLUE SCHOLARS

SINGLE: "50 THOUSAND DEEP"

RECORD: BAYANI

RELEASED: 2007 | **RECORDED IN:** SEATTLE

PRODUCER: SABZI | **LABEL:** MASS LINE MEDIA, RAWKUS RECORDS

The Seattle WTO protests began on November 30, 1999, and the crisis lasted several days, concluding on December 3. The protests were a demonstration against the World Trade Organization Ministerial Conference, then taking place at the Washington State Convention and Trade Center. It was a bloody, dangerous, significant moment in local history.

Fast forward three years: two Seattle-area artists come together to create the Blue Scholars, a hip-hop group focusing on themes of socioeconomics, youth empowerment, and systemic racism. A little backstory: While attending the University of Washington, George Quibuyen (known both as MC Geologic and Prometheus Brown) and Alexei Saba Mohajerjasbi (a.k.a. DJ Sabzi)—also known for his work in the group Common Market—first met at a meeting for the Student Hip-Hop Organization of Washington. The group was born decades earlier in the Bronx and worked to promote and develop a network for students interested in the creative culture.

The rest is history: As the Blue Scholars, Quibuyen and Mohajerjasbi have shared stages with artists like De La Soul and Slick Rick. In 2006, the duo was awarded Best Hip-Hop Artist, Best Local Single, and Best Album in the city by the *Seattle Weekly*. They released the song "Slick Watts" in 2011, an ode to the headband-wearing former Seattle SuperSonics player.

The son of Filipino immigrants, Quibuyen remains an advocate for his community, founding Filipino bakery Hood Famous with Chera Amlag. Iranian-American Mohajerjasbi studied jazz piano and has since expressed how his work with local youth has inspired much of his music. To wit: "50 Thousand Deep" is a song about the WTO protests and the activism and persistence in the Blue Scholars' ongoing fight for equity and a better world for those pushed to the margins. Like much of the best hip-hop music, "50 Thousand Deep" educates its listeners about a historical event from the point of view of a common citizen, a perspective that might otherwise be lost or overshadowed by traditional history books.

ABNEY PARK

SINGLE: "SLEEP ISABELLA"

RECORD: LOST HORIZONS

RELEASED: 2008 | **RECORDED IN:** SEATTLE

PRODUCER: ROBERT BROWN

LABEL: POST-APOCALYPSE RECORDS

The world of rock and roll is large, with many subgenres. Take steampunk, for instance. This style leans into science fiction and fantasy, often incorporating Victorian and American Wild West imagery. In the lyrics of steampunk, it's not surprising to find flying, steam-powered cars, six-shooter shoot-outs in the clouds, and a lexicon that might make you think you're at Comic-Con as much as you are a concert. That's the beauty of the songs.

One of the most beloved steampunk bands in the world hails from Seattle. Formed officially by frontman Robert Brown in 1997, the project, named after a cemetery in London, didn't find its stride in its now-signature genre until around 2005. That's when Brown, who was born in Pullman, Washington, in 1970, took on the moniker Captain Brown

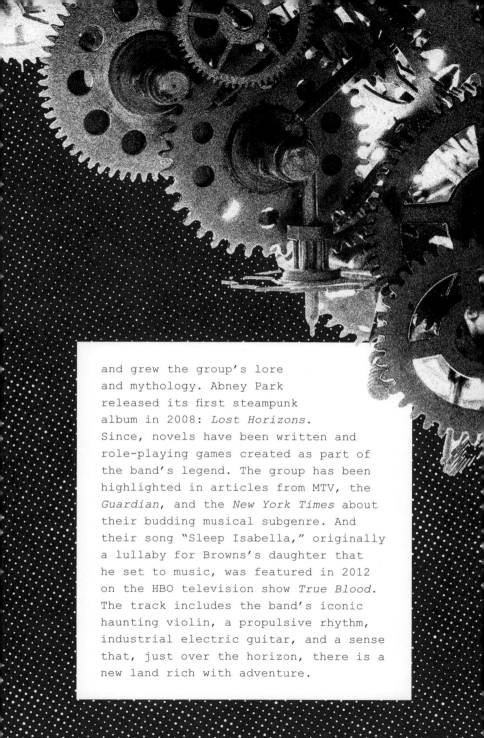

and grew the group's lore
and mythology. Abney Park
released its first steampunk
album in 2008: *Lost Horizons*.
Since, novels have been written and
role-playing games created as part of
the band's legend. The group has been
highlighted in articles from MTV, the
Guardian, and the *New York Times* about
their budding musical subgenre. And
their song "Sleep Isabella," originally
a lullaby for Browns's daughter that
he set to music, was featured in 2012
on the HBO television show *True Blood*.
The track includes the band's iconic
haunting violin, a propulsive rhythm,
industrial electric guitar, and a sense
that, just over the horizon, there is a
new land rich with adventure.

FLEET FOXES

SINGLE: "WHITE WINTER HYMNAL"

RECORD: FLEET FOXES

RELEASED: 2008 | **RECORDED IN:** SEATTLE

PRODUCER: PHIL EK | **LABEL:** SUB POP RECORDS

Fleet Foxes have set up shop at the crossroads between delicate and chilling, making it altogether appropriate that their breakout song was "White Winter Hymnal" from the group's 2008 self-titled debut LP (a Sub Pop release). The Seattle-born group is like the Beach Boys if that band never lived in sunny California and instead lived in rainy Ballard. Fleet Foxes, which were first called the less elegant the Pineapples before finding out another local band had the moniker, formed in 2006 and are led by songwriter and frontman Robin Pecknold. The band's original lineup also included Skyler Skjelset on guitar, Casey Wescott on keys, Bryn Lumsden on bass, and Nicholas Peterson on drums. Over the years, though, the lineup has changed. For several years, it included Josh Tillman, who would play from 2008 to 2012 before breaking off solo and becoming Father John Misty.

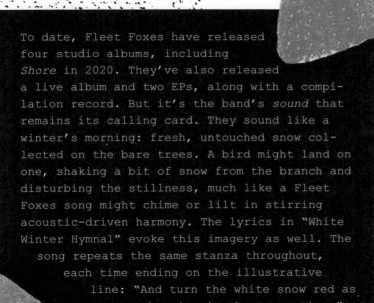

To date, Fleet Foxes have released
four studio albums, including
Shore in 2020. They've also released
a live album and two EPs, along with a compilation record. But it's the band's *sound* that
remains its calling card. They sound like a
winter's morning: fresh, untouched snow collected on the bare trees. A bird might land on
one, shaking a bit of snow from the branch and
disturbing the stillness, much like a Fleet
Foxes song might chime or lilt in stirring
acoustic-driven harmony. The lyrics in "White
Winter Hymnal" evoke this imagery as well. The
song repeats the same stanza throughout,
each time ending on the illustrative
line: "And turn the white snow red as
strawberries in the summertime."
The song, with
the artful stop-
motion music
video, has gone
on to signify
the group's shim-
mering, animated
power.

NISSIM BLACK
(A.K.A. D. BLACK)

SINGLE: "KEEP ON GOING"

RECORD: ALI'YAH

RELEASED: 2009 | **RECORDED IN:** SEATTLE

PRODUCER: D. BLACK, B. BROWN, VITAMIN D, JAKE ONE

LABEL: SPORTN' LIFE RECORDS

Born Damian Jamohl Black, rapper Nissim Black is the son of two Seattle hip-hop pioneers, rappers Mia Black and James "Captain Crunch" Croone of the Emerald Street Girls and Emerald Street Boys, respectively. Black's grandparents were also musical peers of legends Quincy Jones and Ray Charles. Although he endured a difficult childhood, which included time around drugs and gangs, Black has risen above his circumstance to create music with an early mentor and skilled rapper and producer in his own right, Vitamin D (born Derrick Brown).

As a teen, Black began working with local Sportn' Life Records. His first release with the label was a "split vinyl," a record featuring a different group on each side of the single.

He shared the record with the group the Last Men Standing. Not long after, at eighteen years old, the lyricist replaced his father as the co-CEO of Sportn' Life, working with label partner DeVon Manier. Under the moniker D. Black, the rapper released his second studio album *Ali'yah* in 2009, which charted for five weeks on the College Media Journal hip-hop charts. That same year, Black was a candidate to portray Notorious B.I.G. in the biopic *Notorious*, but the role eventually went to Biggie's son, C. J. Wallace. (As of this writing, Black is working with HBO on a comedy series about his life.)

Black turned his attention to education and stopped making music in 2011, during which time he also focused on his conversion to Orthodox Judaism, a transformation long in the making. His song "Keep on Going," which features his friend Vitamin D and is on the *Ali'yah* album, describes the hardships and obstacles Black Americans face in everyday American society. The song's lyrics aim to inspire people to keep moving and pushing through barriers put up against Black Americans. It's a modern-day "We Shall Overcome," a track that encourages its listeners to stop the violence and stay persistent, even when the road is full of hardships and institutional biases put in place to prevent the advancement of people of color.

DAVE MATTHEWS BAND

SINGLE: "FUNNY THE WAY IT IS"

RECORD: BIG WHISKEY & THE GROOGRUX KING

RELEASED: 2009 | **RECORDED IN:** SEATTLE; LOS ANGELES; CHARLOTTESVILLE, VA; NEW ORLEANS; NEW YORK CITY

PRODUCER: JOHN ALAGÍA | **LABEL:** RCA

Before he was a musician of major note, Dave Matthews was an actor in Charlottesville, Virginia. But he summoned up the courage to give some demo tapes to musicians he admired in the college town, from drummer Carter Beauford to guitar player Tim Reynolds. They were in. With a band intact, Matthews began playing colleges and growing an audience. The group helped popularize the '90s jam band boom with its signature combination of saxophone, violin, and Matthews's elastic voice.

Famous for albums like *Under the Table* and *Dreaming* in 1994 and *Crash* in 1996, Dave Matthews Band has released ten studio albumns to date, including *Walk Around the Moon* in 2023. Since the early 2000s, the South African-born Matthews has called Seattle home. He has recorded much of his most recent albums in places like Seattle's Electrokitty and Studio

Litho, kicking things off with the Grammy Award-winning band's 2009 album, *Big Whiskey & the GrooGrux King*, inspired by the untimely death of the band's saxophonist LeRoi Moore.

That album features the sticky single "Funny the Way It Is," an acoustic-driven, radio-friendly track that benefits from Beauford's nimble, prolific drumming, Matthews's frenetic guitar playing, and the band's general sense of joyous rhythms. The album nabbed two Grammy nominations and, like nearly all of DMB's records, debuted at No. 1 on the Billboard 200.

Matthews, whose outfit is one of the highest-grossing live acts of all time, often performs solo for charity, like his recent collaboration with local Tomo Nakayama for the healthcare organization, S.M.A.S.H. For Seattleites, it's become something of a custom to share at parties those rare moments when Matthews has been spotted around town.

The
2010s

MARY LAMBERT ON THE COLLABORATIVE 2010s

When Mary Lambert thinks back on her time coming up in Seattle, she remembers her friends first. Around the turn of the 2010s, Lambert says, there was a prevailing sense among the many talented artists that she knew and collaborated with that a rising tide helped all boats. It was this mentality that fused bonds between artists. In Ballard, for example, via the many open mics and venues, the Head and the Heart blossomed. And in Capitol Hill another act was rising up: Macklemore & Ryan Lewis. Lambert collaborated with the hip-hop duo and became globally famous and socially impactful, thanks to the song "Same Love" on the Grammy Award–winning album *The Heist*. But even with all the accolades and acknowledgments, Lambert is grateful most of all that her friends believed in her.

"For me," says Lambert, "the best barometer, the best metric of success is the idea that the people I respect and am in community with like my shit. That they like and respect me and want to collaborate with me. That feels like success to me."

But Lambert isn't the only one who came up at this time

who feels that way. Indeed, for many, it was a way of life. To wit, Lambert thinks about her friend and collaborator Hollis Wong-Wear. The two formed a friendship in their teens in the local arts organization Youth Speaks Seattle, along with this book's coauthor Eva Walker. (Rapper Travis Thompson is another alum who came out of the impactful organization some years later.) Wong-Wear was a "connector," she says, someone who put on shows, networking functions, and more. And it was Wong-Wear who rose to fame with her performance on the Macklemore & Ryan Lewis song "White Walls," who brought Lambert into the studio one day to record the "Same Love" chorus. The track would later become part of the unofficial soundtrack for LGBTQ+ rights like marriage equality.

"When Hollis called me to do 'Same Love,' I'd just graduated from college," says Lambert. "I was waiting tables in Alki, bartending in Belltown. I worked downtown as a barista. It was a really bonkers time. It was weird I even had a day off."

The call was emblematic of the times. *If I win, you win.* In fact, that philosophy might have been a key to *The Heist*'s success. Each track featured one local standout after another, from Allen Stone to Lambert to Wong-Wear and Ben Bridwell. It was a local greatest hits album of the 2010s as much as anything else. For Lambert, the opportunity to work with Macklemore & Ryan Lewis changed her life. But it was also the result of a lot of hard work and dealing with many highs and lows. Lambert worked as a musician and also as a poet, often competing in slam showcases. She attended Cornish College of the Arts. She endured some of the worst of life and had stories to tell.

"There's so many great storytellers in Seattle," she says. "That's a really common thread here. It's what drew me into working with [Macklemore] too. What I loved so much about 'Same Love.' I think there's an edge of honesty in Seattle too—I mean, think about Kurt."

Growing up, Lambert learned about music from her mother, a singer-songwriter in her own right. Lambert began writing songs around six years old and always knew she wanted to be a performer. While pursuing music seemed impossible at times, she nevertheless began to study it, intending to teach middle school orchestra. At Cornish, she was inspired by a community of vibrant, inventive artists, like Thunderpussy's Molly Sides, world-renowned accordionist Jamie Maschler, composer-performer Maiah Manser, *America's Got Talent* finalist Jimmie Herrod, and experimental harpist Melissa Achten-Klausner.

Today, Lambert is an icon to many, providing the voice to a major shift in society toward legalized gay marriage. It's an almost unimaginable reality for someone who'd felt so much pain for growing up gay, to find herself performing with Madonna and helping to marry same-sex couples on MTV. Carrying on the tradition of queer artists in the city that includes many, including drag icons and musicians of all styles.

"Having my career shaped largely around aspects of my life or identity that have felt shameful or wrong has been gratifying and healing," Lambert says. "To know that people are looking to me, taking my workshop courses, listening to my music as this salve for queer longing—that's really special."

▲ Conor Byrne Pub, a popular venue for local musicians like the Head and the Heart, Seattle, 2023

JAKE ONE

SINGLE: "KNOW WHAT I MEAN"

RECORD: THE STIMULUS PACKAGE (W/ FREEWAY)

RELEASED: 2010 | **RECORDED IN:** SEATTLE

PRODUCER: JAKE ONE | **LABEL:** RHYMESAYERS ENTERTAINMENT

Seattle is known for hip-hop stars like Sir Mix-a-Lot, Ishmael Butler, and Macklemore. But there's another artist flying well below the radar, a person who has created some of the most popular beats in rap history—producer Jake One (a.k.a. "Snare Jordan"). Born Jacob Dutton, the humble musician grew up in Seattle, first in the Central District and then the North End, attending the University of Washington. Since then, he's worked with 50 Cent and G-Unit, Brother Ali, De La Soul, Freeway, Slug of Atmosphere, T. I., Snoop Dogg, Pitbull, J Cole, Drake, Macklemore, Rick Ross, and Chance the Rapper among others. *Phew!*

Jake released his debut solo LP, *White Van Music*, in 2008 (on Rhymesayers) and in 2010 he dropped *The Stimulus Package* with Philadelphia rapper Freeway. Their single, "Know What I Mean," opens with a heavy beat and a crashing snare. Tortured vocal samples swing in like a prayer. Freeway, gravely voiced with a quick, percussive flow, bounces and dances on the music. The album was mixed by legendary local producer Vitamin D and also features guest vocalists like Raekwon of the Wu-Tang Clan.

But Jake, extensive resume and all, is also known around town for his generosity and how closely he keeps an eye and ear out for local rap stand-outs. He's not just collaborating with the Weeknd and Wale. He's also working with Northwest art-ists like Travis Thompson, Dave B., Sol, and Parisalexa. Game recognize game. But Jake, who regularly releases his popular "Behind the Beat" videos on YouTube, is not one to flaunt his achievements with pomp and confetti. Instead, he's the one hanging out in the back of the room, observing and filing away details to use as compo-nents for his next track.

THE HEAD AND THE HEART

SINGLE: "RIVERS AND ROADS"

RECORD: THE HEAD AND THE HEART

RELEASED: 2011 | **RECORDED IN:** SEATTLE

PRODUCER: JSHAWN SIMMONS, THE HEAD AND THE HEART

LABEL: SUB POP RECORDS

Seattle's Ballard neighborhood rocks. Literally. A string of music clubs, including the Sunset Tavern, Tractor Tavern, and Conor Byrne Pub, stretches out along Ballard Avenue. It's in that last spot where Josiah Johnson and Jonathan Russell met at the pub's weekly open mic night and formed their now-famous musical bond. Together, the two started the Head and the Heart in a fever dream of late nights, songwriting, and performing. As the group came into focus with Charity Rose Thielen, Chris Zasche, Kenny Hansley, and Tyler Williams, the band began selling burned demo CDs in handmade denim sleeves. Stores couldn't keep them in stock. And the labels came a-calling, with the *Seattle Times* dubbing it a "feeding frenzy." The Head and the Heart kept things local, eventually signing with Sub Pop Records, which released its self-titled debut LP.

Fans of the band have likely looked up the group's signature song, "Rivers and Roads," which was written by Johnson in a haze somewhere around 3 a.m. If so, they've likely seen the live acoustic rendition on YouTube at the Doe Bay Resort on Orcas Island. (The track's studio recording has since been used in a number of network television shows.) There, you can see the band together, before fame and fortune took hold. (Johnson would eventually go on a multi-year hiatus for personal reasons with Matt Gervais stepping in. As of this writing, though, Johnson is beginning to play with the group more.) It's a beautiful video, shot against the waters of the Salish Sea, no river or road in sight.

To date, the group has released five studio LPs, including *Every Shade of Blue* in 2022. But it's that live Doe Bay video that offers the band in its most essential form, fancy-free and harmonizing like a collection of songbirds.

SHABAZZ PALACES

SINGLE: "FREE PRESS AND CURL"

RECORD: BLACK UP

RELEASED: 2011 | **RECORDED IN:** GUNBEAT SERENADE STUDIO IN

OUTPLACE PALACELANDS

PRODUCER: KNIFE KNIGHTS | **LABEL:** SUB POP RECORDS

A Seattle native, Ishmael Butler has made a name for himself at home and around the world. His musical journey started on alto sax, which he played in his middle school jazz band, and progressed from there to chart high on Billboard. After graduating from Garfield High School in 1987, Butler packed his bags and headed for the East Coast. He first moved to Massachusetts to attend college, where he played division-one basketball at the University of Massachusetts under acclaimed coach John Calipari. Later, Butler would befriend Craig Irving and Mary Ann Vieira, and the trio would form the now-iconic East Coast hip-hop group, Digable Planets. Their biggest hit, "Rebirth of Slick (Cool Like Dat)," peaked at No. 15 on the Billboard Hot 100 and won a Grammy Award for Best Rap Performance by a Duo or Group. In total, Digable Planets released only two albums before disbanding in the mid-1990s.

Butler returned to Seattle in 2003 and six years later formed Shabazz Palaces, part of

the influential Black Constellation collective,
along with artists like Stas THEE Boss and Erik
Blood. After two albums, Shabazz Palaces signed
to Sub Pop Records, where Butler is now an A &
R rep. Shabazz Palaces released their debut on
the label, *Black Up*, in 2011. It is produced by
Knife Knights, the moniker of the musical partnership between Butler and producer and musician
Erik Blood. The album also features vocals from
THEESatisfaction, a duo discovered for their work
with Butler and co. The track "Free Press and
Curl" is an abstract, far-out offering that, like a
galaxy, gives imaginations new places to explore.

A NOTE ON
BLACK
CONSTELLATION

When it comes to music, collaboration doesn't just occur in song; it can also come by way of community. Case in point: Black Constellation. The robust artist collective emerged in the early 2010s in Seattle and its members espouse ideas of expression, experimentation, cosmology, Afrofuturism, expansive thinking, and good old-fashioned beat making. Their union is more like an ongoing creative salon than a traditional band, with artists sharing ideas, beats, rhymes, poetry, theories, and theologies.

Comprised of Shabazz Palaces, rapper and DJ Stas THEE Boss, producer Erik Blood, producer and songwriter OCnotes, rapper Porter Ray, vocalist JusMoni, and musician Nicholas Galanin, Black Constellation also includes visual and literary artists Maikoiyo Alley-Barnes and Nep Sidhu.

In the spring of 2022, KEXP honored the collective with a 10-part podcast, *Fresh Off the Spaceship*, highlighting the members, their music, and philosophies. At the center of Black Constellation is rapper and free spirit Ishmael Butler. The frontman of the Grammy–winning hip-hop group Digable Planets, Butler is as much a sonic shaman as he is a songwriter. His ethereal hip-hop group Shabazz Palaces (which he formed in Seattle) released its debut album, *Black Up*, in 2011. And as KEXP put it in their podcast, that record was the big bang for the celestial musical rap movement to come, as well as Black Constellation.

The life of an artist can be lonesome—friendship, commiseration, dialogue, and support can keep one afloat and on task. Mix that together with conversations about outer space, along with sharing works of Afrofuturism, poetry, and theology, and you have the sublime, vital collective known as Black Constellation.

GRIEVES

SINGLE: "ON THE ROCKS"

RECORD: TOGETHER/APART

RELEASED: 2011 | **RECORDED IN:** NEW YORK CITY; SEATTLE;

FORT COLLINS, CO

PRODUCER: GRIEVES, BUDO | **LABEL:** RHYMESAYERS ENTERTAINMENT

It was sometime in middle school when
Benjamin Laub (a.k.a. Grieves) first experienced the music of Wu-Tang Clan and heard
what sounded like his dad's record collection
sampled throughout. The music he grew up with
and appreciated was being mashed, twisted,
and turned into something new, a common
method in hip-hop (known as "chopping") that
first drew him to the genre. It was in that
moment that Laub was inspired to take the
music he heard as a young kid and refashion
whatever he wanted, reweaving it in his own
hip-hop tracks.

Laub is no stranger to drawing from unusual
inspiration for his songs. He is vocal about
his love for '60s folk songwriters like Bob
Dylan and Carole King, and the freedom that
hip-hop offers. In the genre, beats can be
influenced by folk, classic, soul, jazz, anything really. Born in Chicago, Laub moved to
Washington state to attend college
in Olympia in the early

2000s. He later befriended a few local rappers
and linked up with local label Seven Hills.
That's when he decided to transfer schools so
that he could live in Seattle proper.

In 2008, Grieves connected and began working
with the producer and multi-instrumentalist
Budo, who has since worked extensively with
Macklemore. The team of Grieves and Budo produced two Billboard-charting albums. Grieves'
third studio release, *Together/Apart*—his
second with Budo—peaked at No. 106 on the
Billboard 200. The album's single, "On the
Rocks," offers listeners a look into Grieves's
singing voice, rather than his rapping. He
performs over descending, staccato, almost
disco-like piano chords. And the music video
for the song features comedian and former
Saturday Night Live cast member Kyle Mooney.

SOL

SINGLE: "NEED YOUR LOVE"

RECORD: YOURS TRULY

RELEASED: 2012 | **RECORDED IN:** SEATTLE

PRODUCER: SOL MORAVIA-ROSENBERG, JONNY SIKOV-CASTELLANO

LABEL: SELF-RELEASED

One of Seattle's most entertaining MCs, Sol (born Sol Moravia-Rosenberg) was raised in the city by public school teacher parents. Sol's first attempt at rapping came in middle school with his cousin, Ben Fodor, who later in life would come to be known as Phoenix Jones, a mixed martial artist and Seattle's real-life superhero (costume, cape, and all). Later, Sol, known for his fluid and even effervescent rhymes, developed his craft at the Undercaste Studio in North Seattle, an establishment dedicated to developing the art of recording and championing music like hip-hop, EDM, and R & B.

Sol attended the University of Washington, graduating in 2011 and receiving a grant that gave him the opportunity to travel the globe for ten months. The trip around the world came shortly after he released his 2012 sophomore LP, *Yours Truly*. The record was met with acclaim—it hit No. 1 in the United States on the iTunes Hip-Hop Album chart and clocked in at No. 4 worldwide.

The album also earned a spot on Billboard's Heatseekers Albums chart, peaking at No. 24 in February 2012.

After the release of *Yours Truly*, Sol embarked on a spring West Coast tour. He performed at the Sasquatch! Music Festival in May and headlined one of Seattle's most prestigious venues, the Showbox at the Market, to a sold-out crowd. Afterward, Sol (a.k.a. Solzilla) left on his ten-month world adventure in June of 2012, garnering new inspirations along the way. The artist's song, "Need Your Love," features vocal powerhouse Ray Dalton (of Macklemore's "Can't Hold Us" fame) and violinist Andrew Joslyn, a composer and musician whose work has appeared on countless records. The love song showcases the softer side of rap, through its lovely string arrangement, steady beat, and Sol's smooth style.

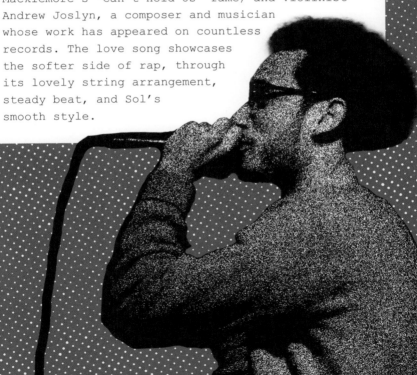

THEESATISFACTION

SINGLE: "QUEENS"

RECORD: AWE NATURALE

RELEASED: 2012 | **RECORDED IN:** SEATTLE

PRODUCER: THEESATISFACTION | **LABEL:** SUB POP RECORDS

It was 1996 when Stasia "Stas" Irons (a.k.a. Stas THEE Boss) moved to Seattle from Tacoma to attend the University of Washington, and it was 1997 when Catherine "Cat" Harris-White (a.k.a. SassyBlack) moved from Hawaii to Seattle, later attending Cornish College of the Arts. Despite attending different schools, the two eventually met in 2005. Three years later, they officially formed THEESatisfaction in 2008 and began to self-release music via Bandcamp.

Not long after, the duo collaborated with acts like Champagne Champagne and Shabazz Palaces. In 2011, THEESatisfaction signed to Sub Pop Records and a year later, they released their first studio album on the label, *Awe Naturale*. The fourth track on the album is the very catchy "QueenS." The song starts with what sounds like a cosmic pulsar, followed

by claps on the two and four and
chants of *ooh-ah-ooh-ah*, leading the
track into what becomes a universe
full of sound. It is like a journey of
rhythmic meditation. First comes the
concentration of thought, then Irons's
trusting voice enters, the listener's guide to bliss and cosmic explo-
ration. Then your ear is led to the
song's chorus where Harris-White takes
over, bringing you closer to euphoria.
Together, the two vocalists take you
on a three-minute journey, creating a
luscious Afrofuturist reality. Sadly,
THEESatisfaction disbanded in 2016,
going their separate ways to pursue
solo careers.

ALLEN STONE

SINGLE: "UNAWARE"

RECORD: ALLEN STONE

RELEASED: 2012 | **RECORDED IN:** SEATTLE

PRODUCER: ANDREW ROSE, LIOR GOLDENBERG | **LABEL:** ATO RECORDS

To hear Allen Stone sing is to believe in a higher power. Stone's voice is hypnotic, angelic, not for any warble or vocal tricks, but for its sparkle and proximity to perfection. Born in tiny Chewelah, Washington, Stone moved to Spokane at eighteen and later to Seattle. He grew up singing in the church, discovering soul music as a teenager. Stone has transcended his humble beginnings and become one of the most elegant singers in popular music.

His song "Unaware" has become his signature. Whether admiring his performance of it in a YouTube video shot in his mother's living room or watching him duet the song with an aspiring artist on *American Idol*, listeners have found "Unaware" is a slow-burn classic. A song about betrayal from a loved one, it has grown in popularity along with Stone's career.

While Stone has released a handful of LPs, including *APART* in 2021, his self-titled

debut LP, re-released nation-
ally by ATO Records in 2012,
was his first brush with star-
dom. The album charted at
No. 35 on the Billboard Top
R & B/Hip-Hop Albums chart
and No. 4 on the Heatseekers
Albums chart. It features
other standout tracks like
"Sleep," "Celebrate Tonight,"
"What I've Seen," and
"Contact High."

Often seen with big-rimmed
eyeglasses, long flowing
blond hair, a blond beard,
and a hat, Stone—featured on
the Macklemore & Ryan Lewis
Grammy-nominated album, *The
Heist*—is an important, heav-
enly voice in the world of
soul music, just as he is an
important figure in Seattle's
sonic pastiche.

MINUS THE BEAR

SINGLE: "STEEL AND BLOOD"

RECORD: INFINITY OVERHEAD

RELEASED: 2012 | **RECORDED IN:** SEATTLE

PRODUCER: MATT BAYLES, MINUS THE BEAR | **LABEL:** DANGERBIRD

Minus the Bear played its first show three days after 9/11 at a venue called the Paradox and played its final tour in 2018 (it released a live album from those gigs called *Farewell*). Everything on that last string of tour dates ended with three sold-out nights at the Showbox in hometown Seattle. In between, the group made significant waves.

Formed by members of different bands like Botch and Kill Sadie, the group was a fixture on MTV in the early 2000s with their music video for the song "Pachuca Sunrise," and they opened for iconic grunge band Soundgarden in 2010. In total, the at times dreamy, at times experimental rock band released six LPs and four EPs throughout its seventeen years. The group's final lineup included Jake Snider on vocals, Dave Knudson on guitar, Cory Murchy on bass, and Alex Rose on synths. Humorously, their band name is something of an inside joke, stemming from a night when one of the members asked a friend of the band how a date had gone.

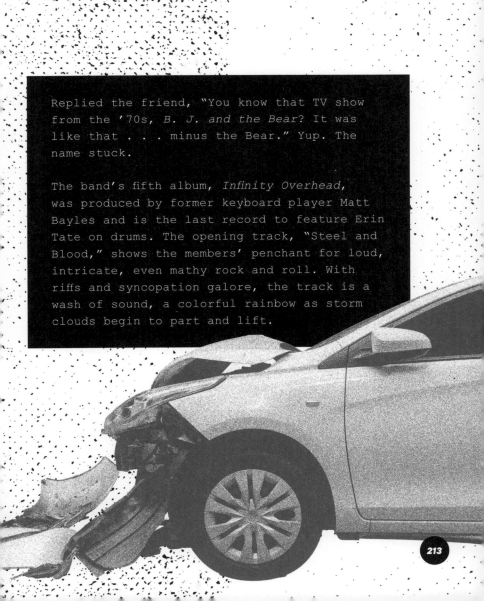

Replied the friend, "You know that TV show from the '70s, *B. J. and the Bear*? It was like that . . . minus the Bear." Yup. The name stuck.

The band's fifth album, *Infinity Overhead*, was produced by former keyboard player Matt Bayles and is the last record to feature Erin Tate on drums. The opening track, "Steel and Blood," shows the members' penchant for loud, intricate, even mathy rock and roll. With riffs and syncopation galore, the track is a wash of sound, a colorful rainbow as storm clouds begin to part and lift.

MACKLEMORE & RYAN LEWIS

SINGLE: "THRIFT SHOP"

RECORD: THE HEIST

RELEASED: 2012 | **RECORDED IN:** SEATTLE

PRODUCER: RYAN LEWIS | **LABEL:** SELF-RELEASED

Simply put, "Thrift Shop" was a phenomenon.

Upon its release, Seattle's Macklemore (born Ben Haggerty) and Ryan Lewis were the talk of the global pop and rap music scenes. The lyricist (Macklemore) was often seen sporting a giant fur coat and signature haircut with shaved sides while his counterpart, Lewis, remained stoically in the background, the knowing inventor of the beat.

The first years of the new millennium were marked by recession in America. It was a time when young people turned to Goodwill and away from the Gap. Money was tight. So when "Thrift Shop" hit in the summer of 2012, much of the world could relate to its message of thrifty discovery. It was simultaneously a reflection of the times and lightning in a bottle. And it was just plain fun. Since then, the song has become one of less than a hundred that have been certified RIAA diamond, meaning more than ten million units were purchased.

"Thrift Shop" features that indelible, quirky saxophone line (that took dozens of drafts to write)—*duh, duh-duh-Duh-duh, duh, dey-err*. Combining Macklemore's irreverent rhyming and the deep-voiced, tag-poppin' hook from long-time Seattle vocalist Wanz, the song became a smash sensation. The single was one of several from Macklemore & Ryan Lewis's LP *The Heist* to impact the world in a major way. Also on the album: party anthem "Can't Hold Us," the historic "Same Love," and the ambitious "Ten Thousand Hours."

The record also honored the Seattle area like no other, featuring local stand-outs aplenty—from Allen Stone to Owuor Arunga to Hollis Wong-Wear—on almost every track. In later years, Mack would work with other artists like Travis Thompson and Reignwolf on solo work. Today, the locally shot music video for "Thrift Shop" (which features many local faces) boasts nearly two billion views on YouTube alone. It's a time capsule—like the clothes and objects it highlights—as much as it is a straight-up earworm.

LA LUZ

SINGLE: "CALL ME IN THE DAY"

RECORD: IT'S ALIVE

RELEASED: 2013 | **RECORDED IN:** SEATTLE

PRODUCER: LA LUZ, JOHNNY GOSS | **LABEL:** HARDLY ART

When you hear the words *surf noir*, what comes to mind? Surfing in the moonlight? Dark abandoned beaches featured in old movie reels or maybe a black-and-white murder mystery on the boardwalk?

Any of these would be a fitting backdrop to the sounds produced by Seattle-born band La Luz. Although now based in California, the band was formed in 2012 in the Evergreen State by Shana Cleveland, Alice Sandahl, Marian Li Pino, and Abbey Blackwell. Other members have included Lena Simon and Audrey Johnson. Inspired by the music of acts like Link Wray, the Shirelles, Dick Dale, and guitarist Takeshi Terauchi, La Luz signed to Sub Pop's sister label, Hardly Art, after their first EP *Damp Face* released in 2012.

In 2013, the burgeoning group dropped their debut full-length album, *It's Alive*. While on tour later that same year, the band was involved in a serious automobile accident on their way to Seattle from Boise. Their tour van drove over black ice, causing it to slide and crash into the divider on the road. That's when a semi-truck struck the van,

destroying the vehicle, as well as the instru-
ments and gear inside, and causing bad bruises.
The band had to cancel the rest of the tour with
Of Montreal.

La Luz was back up and running a few months later,
releasing the acclaimed *Weirdo Shrine* in 2015.
To date, La Luz has worked with artists such as
Ty Segal, who produced *Weirdo Shrine*, and Adrian
Younge, who produced the band's self-titled 2021
release. Their sound, which was even featured in a
Miller Lite commercial, is born from eerie harmonies and Cleveland's at times vaudevillian sense
of humor. The single "Call Me in the Day" is the
quintessential combination of '60s doo-wop, psychedelic rock, and the feeling of walking on a
deserted beach under twinkling blue stars. Surf
noir, indeed.

INDUSTRIAL REVELATION

SINGLE: "SAYING GOODBYE
(TO RAINBOW SOCKS AND HAIR DYE)"

RECORD: OAK HEAD

RELEASED: 2013 | **RECORDED IN:** PORT LUDLOW, WA

PRODUCER: DAVE ABRAMSON, INDUSTRIAL REVELATION

LABEL: SELF-RELEASED

The instrumental band's debut album *Oak Head* is, well, perfect. It's the product of four world-class musicians at the top of their games, including bassist Evan Flory-Barnes, the composer of the melodic, reflective "Saying Goodbye (To Rainbow Socks and Hair Dye)," the final track on *Oak Head*. Flory-Barnes is also the author of the magnificent bassline to the Macklemore & Ryan Lewis hit "Downtown." The band's keyboardist Josh Rawlings is also a regular M&RL collaborator, a masterful keyboard and piano player. Trumpeter Ahamefule J. Oluo, creator of the hit stage show *Now I'm Fine*, sings through his horn. And drummer and band founder D'Vonne Lewis keeps everything packed and on track, yet still somehow bouncing. Together,

Industrial Revelation is a Voltron-like collection making something greater than the sum of its parts (a staggering statement considering the resumes and abilities of the four).

The band won a coveted Genius Award from Seattle alternative newspaper *The Stranger* after the release of its 8-track debut LP. The group then released its second LP, *Liberation & the Kingdom of Nri*, in 2015. Since, the prolific members have largely been involved in their own projects, as well as playing in other bands. Lewis, the grandson of Dave Lewis, is a fixture in the jazz scene, one of the most coveted kit players around. Flory-Barnes is a burgeoning solo artist and a wizard on the bass. Rawlings and Oluo are also creating and performing at the highest levels of their crafts. But no matter what, the quartet recorded *Oak Head* in a cabin of the same name outside the city, and it remains a gift to any music lover who chances upon it.

DAMIEN JURADO

SINGLE: "SILVER TIMOTHY"

RECORD: BROTHERS AND SISTERS OF THE ETERNAL SON

RELEASED: 2014 | **RECORDED IN:** COTTAGE GROVE, OR

PRODUCER: RICHARD SWIFT | **LABEL:** SECRETLY CANADIAN

Signed in the mid-1990s to Sub Pop Records at the behest of Sunny Day Real Estate guitar player Jeremy Enigk, Damien Jurado has been something of a quiet star in the city. He released a handful of albums with Sub Pop from 1997 to 2000, and since then he's released dozens of LPs and EPs that showcase his signature lo-fi, stream of consciousness, poetic songwriting. When listening to Jurado, it's like you're reading a letter sent to you from the past. He dreams up his songs . . . literally, as with his 2014 LP *Brothers and Sisters of the Eternal Son* (the sequel to the 2012 album *Maraqopa*). That record centers around a fictional world and protagonist that Jurado conceived of while sleeping. Both albums were produced by the late Richard Swift, who had worked with many important bands, including Fleet Foxes, Pedro the Lion, the Black Keys, and Seattleite and member of the Shins, Yuuki Matthews. Jurado is no stranger to famous collaborators himself, having worked with Father John Misty (whom he helped discover) and Moby.

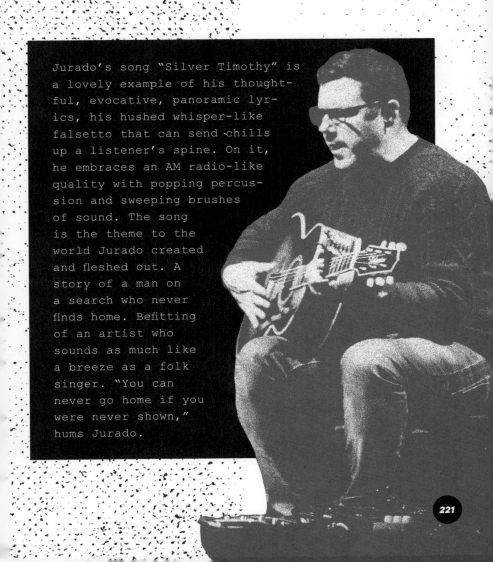

Jurado's song "Silver Timothy" is a lovely example of his thoughtful, evocative, panoramic lyrics, his hushed whisper-like falsetto that can send chills up a listener's spine. On it, he embraces an AM radio-like quality with popping percussion and sweeping brushes of sound. The song is the theme to the world Jurado created and fleshed out. A story of a man on a search who never finds home. Befitting of an artist who sounds as much like a breeze as a folk singer. "You can never go home if you were never shown," hums Jurado.

NIGHTRAIN

SINGLE: "MATING CALL"

RECORD: MATING CALL

RELEASED: 2014 | **RECORDED IN:** SEATTLE

PRODUCER: ERIK BLOOD | **LABEL:** SELF-RELEASED

In 2007, a casting call went out in search of
four Black women who could act in a play about a
fictional group of gals who wanted to form a band,
despite not having much experience. The name of
the fictitious band and musical was Hot Grits. Once
formed, the production hit some road bumps. The
bassist left the group before their upcoming two-
week residency at local club Re-bar. Replacing the
bass player, the group soldiered on. After several
months of jams, lessons, and rehearsals, the
members even began to play original songs.

Though expected to go their separate ways after
the production concluded, they were inspired
to keep a good thing going. Bringing back the
original bassist, the once fictional band became
a reality. The group made it even more official
with a new name, NighTraiN. The core lineup
included Rachael Ferguson on vocals and keyboards,
guitarist Nicole Cherie Peoples, bassist Selena
Whitaker-Paquiet, and Taryn Dorsey on drums.
NighTraiN went on to play myriad shows around
Seattle and, six years after forming, finally
released the debut album *Mating Call*. The LP,

which features the sumptuous title song, sung by Whitaker-Paquiet, was produced by beloved local musician Erik Blood, who met the band at a show they played together in 2013.

In the 2020s, after the group disbanded, members went on to join or support other bands like Fly Moon Royalty, Wiscon, Pink Lotion, and more. Crucially, the group has helped discover and display upcoming musicians in the city, thanks to events like Whitaker-Paquiet's annual summer HoodStock Festival, which has featured artists like Danny Denial, Whitney Mongé, and Shaina Shepherd over the years. NighTraiN's example as a hard rocking all-Black female group is a local inspiration to many, and they have blazed a path for artists like Brittany Davis and TeZATalks.

TACOCAT

SINGLE: "CRIMSON WAVE"

RECORD: NVM

RELEASED: 2014 | **RECORDED IN:** SEATTLE

PRODUCER: CONRAD UNO, TACOCAT | **LABEL:** HARDLY ART

With bright colors, buzzy guitars, and a palindrome for a name, Tacocat has been sprinkling rainbow punk dust throughout the region since 2007. The band consists of Emily Nokes on lead vocals, Eric Randall on guitar, Bree McKenna on bass, and Lelah Maupin on drums. Together, they offer a humorous and sarcastic approach to feminism. That combination is present in songs like "Crimson Wave," "Hey Girl," "Men Explain Things to Me," and more.

It should surprise no one but the band first bonded over their love of the local riot grrrl movement of the early '90s. And it's safe to say today that Tacocat has been continuing this legacy of rebellious energy and sticky punk songs, along with groups like Childbirth and Chastity Belt. To date, Tacocat boasts numerous releases on Sub Pop's Hardly Art label, and the band signed to Sub Pop proper for their 2019 album *This Mess Is a Place*.

Since forming in 2007, Tacocat has built an impressive resume, from

inclusion in the Coachella lineup in 2017 to writing and performing the 2016 theme music for Cartoon Network's *The Powerpuff Girls*. The band has also undertaken many tours across both the United States and Europe. The track "Crimson Wave" is a perfect example of the band's wittiness, subversion, and bubblegum pop punk sound that make them required listening. It's a song about, well, that time of the month, but it's a track that's so well done and catchy that it takes any false ideas of embarrassment out of the equation for all listening.

PERFUME GENIUS

SINGLE: "QUEEN"

RECORD: TOO BRIGHT

RELEASED: 2014 | **RECORDED IN:** BRISTOL, UK

PRODUCER: ADRIAN UTLEY, ALI CHANT | **LABEL:** MATADOR

Words like brash and bold can't contain the brilliance that is Perfume Genius. The artist's music is like a smirk in a cracked vanity mirror. For exhibit A, look no further than the gilded "Queen" from his 2014 LP *Too Bright*. Pristine, brazen production precedes war cries and platinum jewelry. Perfume Genius (born Michael Hadreas) has the confidence most wish to summon when their days are rain soaked and their moods equally dark. Born in Des Moines, Iowa, the artist moved to Seattle with his family as a child. As a young adult, he moved across the country to Brooklyn after receiving threats in school for being the only openly gay student. In 2005, though, he moved back to Seattle and began producing music under one of the coolest musical monikers going.

Just a few years later, Perfume Genius was performing "Queen" on *The Late Show with David Letterman* in a white suit and bright red lipstick, words seemingly emblazoned in neon as he sang. The album *Too Bright*, which he worked on with Portishead guitarist Adrian Utley, was a breakout for Perfume Genius. It's led to a career in which

he's collaborated with the likes of Sharon Van Etten and the Yeah Yeah Yeahs. In 2023, he even earned a Grammy nomination for Best Alternative Music Performance for his vocal feature on Yeah Yeah Yeahs' "Spitting Off the Edge of the World." To date, the musician has released a handful of LPs, including *Ugly Season* in 2022. But it's *Too Bright*, which hit No. 83 on the Billboard Top 200 chart and included standouts like the wilting "I Decline," the forlorn "Don't Let Them In," and the shimmering "Queen," that continues to glimmer like the North Star.

MARY LAMBERT

SINGLE: "SECRETS"

RECORD: HEART ON MY SLEEVE

RELEASED: 2014 | **RECORDED IN:** LOS ANGELES

PRODUCER: BENNY CASSETTE, ERIC ROSSE | **LABEL:** CAPITOL RECORDS

Would you believe it if someone said that, this time next year, you would no longer be working a day job? In fact, instead of clocking in at your regular hour, you'll be "clocking in" at the 56th Annual Grammy Awards, nominated for Song of the Year and Album of the Year. But wait, there's more! You'll also be singing onstage at the awards show with Macklemore & Ryan Lewis and Madonna, while Queen Latifah weds thirty-three couples in what will become one of the most unforgetta-ble moments in the history of the show? Would you believe it?

This fairy tale came true for Everett's Mary Lambert. From the humble beginnings of spoken word poetry at a small café in the University District with Youth Speaks Seattle, Lambert's writing began to be featured in outlets like the Brave New Voices International Poetry Competition, filmed for HBO, as she represented Seattle. Later, she grad-uated from Cornish College of the Arts with the intention of becoming a teacher, but her interest in music became the priority, and applying to grad schools was put on hold. A full year didn't even

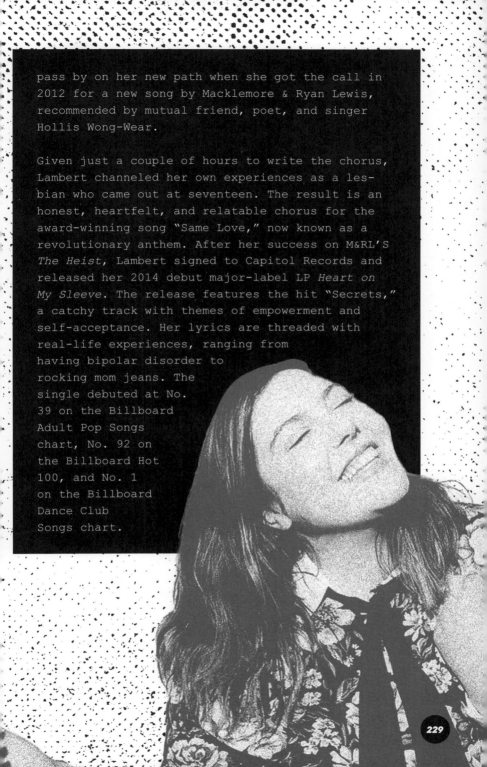

pass by on her new path when she got the call in 2012 for a new song by Macklemore & Ryan Lewis, recommended by mutual friend, poet, and singer Hollis Wong-Wear.

Given just a couple of hours to write the chorus, Lambert channeled her own experiences as a lesbian who came out at seventeen. The result is an honest, heartfelt, and relatable chorus for the award-winning song "Same Love," now known as a revolutionary anthem. After her success on M&RL'S *The Heist*, Lambert signed to Capitol Records and released her 2014 debut major-label LP *Heart on My Sleeve*. The release features the hit "Secrets," a catchy track with themes of empowerment and self-acceptance. Her lyrics are threaded with real-life experiences, ranging from having bipolar disorder to rocking mom jeans. The single debuted at No. 39 on the Billboard Adult Pop Songs chart, No. 92 on the Billboard Hot 100, and No. 1 on the Billboard Dance Club Songs chart.

ODESZA

SINGLE: "LINE OF SIGHT"

RECORD: A MOMENT APART

RELEASED: 2017 | **RECORDED IN:** CHELAN, WA

PRODUCER: HARRISON MILLS, CLAYTON KNIGHT | **LABEL:** COUNTER RECORDS

Formed in 2012 at Western Washington University by two friends, Harrison Mills and Clayton Knight, ODESZA improved and gained a fan base via hours in front of computers as they created their homemade electronic songs from scratch. Quickly, a legion of fans emerged thanks to tracks the duo released. In more recent years, Mills and Knight have been garnering millions more views and selling out venues like Seattle's Climate Pledge Arena several nights in a row. In between, the duo released their 2017 album *A Moment Apart*, their third LP and first in three years.

To write it, the duo rented a cabin near Lake Chelan and experienced a breakthrough, writing three songs in a matter of days. For the duo, a song always begins with something simple, like a piano loop, upon which they build and build worlds and layers. ODESZA called their album *A Moment Apart* because they needed space from the rapid fame and attention they were receiving. The album, which features the likes of Leon Bridges and Regina Spektor, includes the song "Line of Sight." It's a lush, vocal-driven yet percussive song that both heals and balloons the spirit. (There is also an excellent KEXP in-studio version of it on YouTube.)

Today, ODESZA has only grown, headlining at major festivals. The three-time Grammy-nominated electronic group released its acclaimed album *The Last Goodbye* in 2022. We're proud to report that this book's coauthor Eva Walker was featured in the music video for the record's titular lead single, which was also shown at the 2023 Grammy Awards. But it's *A Moment Apart* that elevated ODESZA to a full-fledged global musical force.

COURTNEY MARIE ANDREWS

SINGLE: "MAY YOUR KINDNESS REMAIN"

RECORD: MAY YOUR KINDNESS REMAIN

RELEASED: 2018 | **RECORDED IN:** SEATTLE

PRODUCER: COURTNEY MARIE ANDREWS, MARK HOWARD

LABEL: FAT POSSUM RECORDS

While Courtney Marie Andrews was born in Phoenix, it was in the Seattle-area that she recorded the album that made her a star. Andrews, who connected with Jimmy Eat World frontman Jim Adkins in 2009 for her first big opportunity recording vocals on his Arizona band's rock songs, moved to the PNW in 2011. And it was here where she honed her now-signature Americana songwriting style. In Seattle, Andrews began playing electric guitar for popular local artist Damien Jurado. Several years later in 2018, she released her keen-eyed breakthrough LP, *May Your Kindness Remain*. Soon after, she was opening for Brandi Carlile on tour as a solo act.

Beginning with the heartfelt titular track, the record is a lesson in hard-won wisdom and sharp-minded songwriting. As a result, the album made it onto a number of year-end tastemaker lists. Andrews had officially arrived. Her 2020 follow-up LP, *Old Flowers*, resulted in her first Grammy nomination.

The trajectory of her life was forever altered for the better when she relocated to the PNW those many years ago. Andrews, a fixture at Tractor Tavern in Ballard, took up residence in a rural locale between Duval, Washington and Carnation, Washington, working as a bartender and slowing her pace between tours. Though Andrews is now a Nashville staple, her creative roots run deep in our region.

BRANDI CARLILE

SINGLE: "THE JOKE"

RECORD: BY THE WAY, I FORGIVE YOU

RELEASED: 2018 | **RECORDED IN:** NASHVILLE, TN

PRODUCER: DAVE COBB, SHOOTER JENNINGS | **LABEL:** ELEKTRA

Brandi Carlile's sixth album made her a household name. While she'd earned success with her song "The Story," which was written by longtime collaborator, Seattleite Phil Hanseroth, Carlile earned global acclaim thanks to her 2018 record and its breakout song, "The Joke." Carlile tells the story of the song in her bestselling memoir, *Broken Horses*. The album was otherwise done, but it needed one more track. Producer Dave Cobb pushed her to write a last song. The LP, he said, needed that final dot to the exclamation point. Then in a moment, the lines came to Carlile and she rushed everyone to the studio to record it.

"The Joke" is an uplifting track that says to those who are ridiculed that the joke is *really* on the bully ridiculer. The song won two Grammy Awards and the album it came from won another for good measure.

Today, the Americana/folk rock/alt-country artist with the soaring yet silky voice is a fixture on the world's largest stages. She's also become close friends with the likes of Elton John and

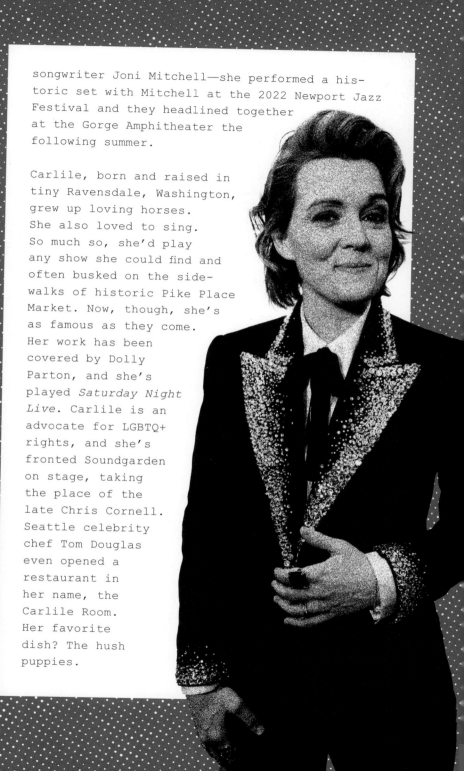

songwriter Joni Mitchell—she performed a historic set with Mitchell at the 2022 Newport Jazz Festival and they headlined together at the Gorge Amphitheater the following summer.

Carlile, born and raised in tiny Ravensdale, Washington, grew up loving horses. She also loved to sing. So much so, she'd play any show she could find and often busked on the sidewalks of historic Pike Place Market. Now, though, she's as famous as they come. Her work has been covered by Dolly Parton, and she's played *Saturday Night Live*. Carlile is an advocate for LGBTQ+ rights, and she's fronted Soundgarden on stage, taking the place of the late Chris Cornell. Seattle celebrity chef Tom Douglas even opened a restaurant in her name, the Carlile Room. Her favorite dish? The hush puppies.

THE
GORGE
754 SILICA ROAD NW, QUINCY

One of the most beautiful concert venues on Earth, the Gorge Amphitheatre, which has spawned way too many "This place is *Gorge*-ous!" puns, is located in George, Washington, about halfway between Seattle and Spokane. The place is an outdoor music oasis where people can camp out, enjoy the sun, and view the bands on stage against the stunning natural backdrop of the Columbia River Gorge. As such, the Gorge has been home to acclaimed festivals—like the local Sasquatch!—and many multi-night stints by artists like Dave Matthews, who has played some seventy shows onsite.

To wit, the "Crash into Me" singer holds an annual three-day event on Labor Day weekend. During Matthews's mini-festival, fans spend several days, all day, listening to DMB and whatever other stellar big-name openers have been tapped for the occasion, including the likes of Brandi Carlile, who has shared the space with Matthews several times. Carlile, too, graced the Gorge stage in 2023 for a "Joni Jam" with iconic artist Joni Mitchell and other artists like Annie Lennox and Sarah McLachlan.

At the Gorge, music lovers can enjoy the sparkling glints of the nearby Columbia River dancing in the distance as rocky hillsides push against the horizon. Music rolls out from the giant stage as upwards of nineteen thousand sit on the grass or in the seats or meander between vendors and merchandise tables. The spot, founded in 1986, originally seated just three thousand. But the concert promoter Live Nation bought the venue in 2006, and it has since hosted big events like Ozzfest, H.O.R.D.E., and Lollapalooza and artists like Pearl Jam, Radiohead, Soundgarden, and even Robert Plant and Jimmy Page. For those who can't make it to the venue, both Pearl Jam and Matthews have released live albums from the Gorge, so you can experience the Gorge vicariously. The venue was also immortalized in 2021 via the acclaimed documentary *Enormous: The Gorge Story*. Today, it remains one of the most picturesque places on earth to enjoy live music.

PARISALEXA

SINGLE: "LIKE ME BETTER"

RECORD: FLEXA

RELEASED: 2018 | **RECORDED IN:** SEATTLE

PRODUCER: ELAN WRIGHT, TYLER DOPPS

LABEL: SELF-RELEASED

Born in New Jersey and raised in Redmond, Washington, Parisalexa has gone on to become a songwriter to the stars. While she has the sound, look, and charisma to be in the spotlight herself, Paris says she relishes the writing process most of all. So much so that she's penned verses for stars like Ciara and Normani. But, she says, if she writes something that's personal enough, Paris will keep it for herself and her own records. The artist, who has released a handful of albums, like *Flexa* in 2018 and *Vroom* in 2021, is smooth as silk when she sings.

Today, Paris lives and works a lot of the time in Los Angeles, a hotbed of creativity and a perfect home for her pop and R & B sensibilities. There, she's focusing on writing solo music as well as new collaborations. With her track record, she shouldn't have any trouble with either. Many, in fact, saw Paris on network television in 2019 when she appeared on the popular competition show *Songland*, impressing judges like Charlie Puth and Ryan Tedder. *Billboard* magazine called her offering on the episode the best of the installment *and* the season.

Indeed, composing has long been a skill for Paris, who fell in love with music before kindergarten. Her 2018 song "Like Me Better," which features the artist Jaz, demonstrates her vocal prowess and her ability to write sticky lines, whether for herself or others.

CAR SEAT HEADREST

SINGLE: "BEACH LIFE-IN-DEATH"

RECORD: TWIN FANTASY (FACE TO FACE)

RELEASED: 2018 | **RECORDED IN:** SEATTLE; CHICAGO

PRODUCER: WILL TOLEDO | **LABEL:** MATADOR RECORDS

The success story of Will Toledo's Virginia-born indie rock project is also a story about the importance of the platform Bandcamp. In 2010, as a teenager, Toledo released his first record, titled *1*, on the music website. That same year, he released albums *2*, *3*, and *4*. And between then and 2018, Car Seat Headrest (named thus because the at times reclusive Toledo would record vocals in the backseat of his car for privacy) released eight more albums, including *Twin Fantasy* in 2011 and *Twin Fantasy (Face to Face)* in 2018.

The latter was a full-band, re-recorded version of the 2011 offering and was released on Matador Records. And the album's "Beach Life-in-Death," shared on Spotify ahead of the album itself, portended the 2018 release. The thirteen-minute song features buzzy guitars, thrashing solos, and Toledo's distorted, bemoaning vocals. The composition is an achievement.

In 2015, Toledo moved from the East Coast to Seattle, where he recruited band members from Craigslist. He's long been savvy when it comes to

technology and the reach of the internet. Even
recently, he put together a new video game with
band member Andrew Katz, in which players engage
online to defeat the jokingly "evil" founder of
Matador Records, Chris Lombardi.

Today, whether touring—Car Seat Headrest even
played Madison Square Garden, backed by Seattle
band Naked Giants—or releasing work on Bandcamp
and elsewhere, it's the group's online following that has carried them to a world beyond the
backseat.

DELVON LAMARR ORGAN TRIO

SINGLE: "CONCUSSION"

RECORD: CLOSE BUT NO CIGAR

RELEASED: 2018 | **RECORDED IN:** SEATTLE

PRODUCER: DELVON LAMARR, DAVID MCGRAW

LABEL: COLEMINE RECORDS

Formed in 2015, the Delvon Lamarr Organ Trio soon began a weekly residency at the popular south Seattle venue the Royal Room. The trio's original lineup included Delvon Lamarr on the Hammond B-3 organ, drummer David McGraw (also of the band the True Loves), and guitarist Colin Higgins. After Higgins's departure, True Loves' guitarist and band leader Jabrille "Jimmy James" Williams joined the group.

The trio's first big break came during Upstream music festival in downtown Seattle, when the group played a warmup set live on KEXP and recorded at the London Plane restaurant. To date, the video of that performance has garnered more than twelve million views on YouTube alone. Songs featured in that set were the band's rendition of the classic "Move on Up" by Curtis Mayfield; "Memphis," which was originally written by John Patton; and another song labeled "Untitled." It was sometime around 2016 when McGraw reached out to Colemine Records and submitted the songs that would later be re-released by the famed label in 2018.

That album, *Close but No Cigar*, hit No. 1 on the US Contemporary Jazz Albums chart and No. 3 on the US Jazz Albums chart, making the band stars. The first track on the record, "Concussion," is a funky tune that displays the band's skill and facility. The track is highlighted by James, who bends guitar notes like Gumby. Lamarr shines on the organ and McGraw is impeccable, moving the song forward one beat at a time.

THUNDERPUSSY

SINGLE: "SPEED QUEEN"

RECORD: THUNDERPUSSY

RELEASED: 2018 | **RECORDED IN:** SEATTLE

PRODUCER: SYLVIA MASSY | **LABEL:** STARDOG RECORDS, REPUBLIC RECORDS

"Thunderpussy" kind of says it all. The energetic all-female rock band is the brainchild of singer Molly Sides and guitarist Whitney Petty. Together, they're joined by bassist Leah Julius and drummer Lindsey Elias. (Former drummers of the group include Lena Simon and Ruby Dunphy.) The group's big break came at the then-annual Sasquatch! Music Festival when Pearl Jam guitarist Mike McCready discovered the rockers onstage, becoming an instant fan. McCready soon released their single "Velvet Noose" on his boutique HockeyTalkter Records label, also providing a dazzling guitar solo on the track.

Inspired by the rock and roll style of the 1970s, Thunderpussy pushes the boundaries of the genre in the modern era with flashy outfits matched with powerhouse instrumentation. Vocalist Sides demands your attention, and she can control a crowd from the front row all the way to the folks climbing in through the windows. Since the group got its start in 2014, Thunderpussy has released several albums, including one produced by renowned engineer Sylvia Massy. The first track off their 2018 self-titled

full-length album, "Speed Queen," is a song kicked
off by Dunphy's masterful rock drums, before
Petty's screeching guitar and Julius's heavy bass
join in. It climaxes with the song's central riff
as Sides's room-filling rock voice hits.

Through persistence, dedication, and showmanship,
Thunderpussy has remained one of Seattle's favorite live bands. It's this power, grind, and hard
work that also led to the group winning a landmark
case in the US Supreme Court, earning the right
to trademark their name. The word isn't dirty, the
band argued. It's essential, powerful, and life
giving, kind of like their music.

DUFF MCKAGAN

SINGLE: "PARKLAND"

RECORD: TENDERNESS

RELEASED: 2019 | **RECORDED IN:** NEW BRIGHTON, UK

PRODUCER: SHOOTER JENNINGS | **LABEL:** UNIVERSAL

Born Michael Andrew McKagan in Seattle on February 5, 1964, prolific musician and songwriter Duff McKagan is best known as the bassist for the incredibly successful rock band Guns N' Roses. But his experience runs deep and wide, as he has led many musical lives. Before dropping out, McKagan attended Roosevelt High School with Anthony Ray (a.k.a. Sir Mix-a-Lot). As a young adult, he played with bands like the Fastbacks, the Fartz, and 10 Minute Warning. He joined Guns N' Roses in 1985 and the group released some of the most popular hard rock songs of the twentieth century, from "Welcome to the Jungle" to "Paradise City."

Since then, he's founded groups like Velvet Revolver and briefly joined others like Alice in Chains and Jane's Addiction. McKagan has written two books (one a *New York Times* bestseller) and was one of the last people to see Nirvana frontman Kurt Cobain before he died, sitting next to him on a flight between L.A. and Seattle after the Nirvana singer left a rehab center early. McKagan also experienced his own issues regarding substance abuse, nearly dying in the mid-1990s. He got sober and has since become much more health conscious.

The songwriter, who has claimed that *The Simpsons'* Duff Beer is named after him, has released a few solo albums in his career—the star-studded rock album *Believe in Me* in 1993, the more reflective *Tenderness* in 2019, and *Lighthouse* in 2023. The idea at first was to create a written follow-up to his 2015 bestselling book, but the former magazine columnist instead made an album, collaborating with budding producer Shooter Jennings. On the song "Parkland," McKagan laments the American problem of gun violence. Nevertheless, the overall album remains hopeful, ending with the resilient "Don't Look Back." Well said, for someone who's seen so much.

TRAVIS THOMPSON

SINGLE: "GLASS CEILING"

RECORD: RECKLESS ENDANGERMENT

RELEASED: 2019 | **RECORDED IN:** SEATTLE

PRODUCER: TYLER DOPPS | **LABEL:** BLVD BOYS/EPIC

Just another day at the pizza shop in Burien, Washington, slinging slices and asking, "Debit or credit?" Well, for some maybe but not for burgeoning rapper Travis Thompson. When he began making music on his sister's laptop, it was in between customers at his job at a local pizzeria, eventually making enough dough for his own recording equipment.

Thompson worked his way into the spotlight, a position he would hide from early in his life. Now, he's garnered millions of streams and video views. Participating in local youth organizations, Thompson started recording music for release at the Macklemore & Ryan Lewis-founded music school, the Residency—or as he called it, "rap camp." Those opportunities led to local music releases and shows, opening for more established acts.

Later, through mutual friend and producer Tyler Dopps, Thompson got a chance to work with Macklemore on a new song. It was that connection that led to the track "Corner Store," from

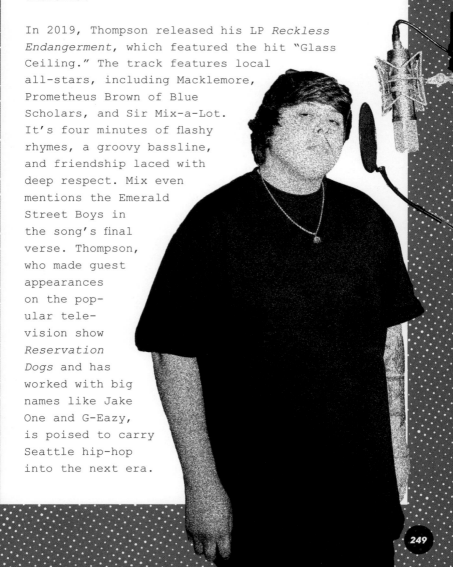

Macklemore's solo LP *Gemini*. It's also a song
the two rappers, with Dave B., would perform live
on *The Tonight Show Starring Jimmy Fallon*. More
recently, Thompson has enjoyed his own success,
with a string of sold-out shows including gigs in
Seattle at venues like the Showbox—and a major
record deal with Epic Records, under the Sony
umbrella.

In 2019, Thompson released his LP *Reckless
Endangerment*, which featured the hit "Glass
Ceiling." The track features local
all-stars, including Macklemore,
Prometheus Brown of Blue
Scholars, and Sir Mix-a-Lot.
It's four minutes of flashy
rhymes, a groovy bassline,
and friendship laced with
deep respect. Mix even
mentions the Emerald
Street Boys in
the song's final
verse. Thompson,
who made guest
appearances
on the pop-
ular tele-
vision show
*Reservation
Dogs* and has
worked with big
names like Jake
One and G-Eazy,
is poised to carry
Seattle hip-hop
into the next era.

The
2020s

NAVIGATING THE 2020S WITH AYRON JONES

For Seattle-born chart-topping rocker Ayron Jones, Seattle offers its artists an essential thing: a proving ground for future success. Some musicians in town, Jones says, can earn a viable living playing gigs and working within the city's scene. Others, sharpened by Seattle and all it has to offer, can go even further, performing and touring on national and international levels (as he has). There's an ecosystem of venues and enough infrastructure that an artist can earn attention in Seattle, grow and spread their wings. That's just what Jones did. As a guitar player coming up in the city in the 2000s and 2010s, Jones played hundreds of shows before he got his big break—the chance to work with Seattle legend Sir Mix-a-Lot.

"Mix brought me into Seattle music circles," he says. Previously, Jones had been playing open mics, cafés, and lounges, along with some club stages. But before Sir Mix-a-Lot reached out and eventually produced Jones's debut independent record, *Dream*, he didn't know how much the city truly had to offer. "For me," says Jones, "it hit me that I was a part of something. I wasn't just some musician coming out of nowhere. I was part of a lineage of music."

If you're a Black lead guitar player like Jones growing up in Seattle, you're going to hear about Jimi Hendrix. You see the murals and the statue, hear the stories. But until you think about the fact you're walking down the same streets he did, the truth might not sink in: Seattle is a place where legends are born. Similarly, getting discovered by Mix in 2012 opened a new world to Jones. He met other local stalwarts like Mike McCready and Duff McKagan. Barrett Martin was a big influence, helping Jones to produce his second album, *Audio Paint Job*, which led to him finding management and his first major label contract. He has since topped the Billboard Mainstream Rock Airplay chart twice with his thrilling, powerful songs "Mercy" and "Blood in the Water."

"For me," Jones says, "what 'the Seattle sound' means is this raw form of rock music. Roots rock with a touch of a dark cloud of depression over the top."

Makes sense. As a kid, Jones

grew up in tough circum-
stances. His parents abandoned
him as a young person, and he
was raised by extended family
members. Music, for which he
long showed an aptitude, was
his "escape," he says. It was
also his way of rising above his
station. Music allowed him to
express himself, connect to an
audience, and strut his stuff.
And it was a way out. Music
offered Jones a chance for more
in the world during a time when
he didn't have nearly as much as
he needed.

"A lot of Black cats deal with
this," says Jones. "Whether
you want to be an athlete or a
comedian or what have you, you
want to be something more than
you've been cast. For me, that
was music."

In the 2010s, as Jones was
beginning to make a name for
himself locally, playing more
shows than likely anyone else
in town, he felt a sense that
anything was possible. Today,
though, it feels somewhat
different in Seattle, he says.
The COVID-19 pandemic at the
turn of the decade affected
much of the city's day-to-day
infrastructure. People are now
often inclined to stay home, and
several venues have shut down,
whereas in the 2010s, post-
grunge, it felt like possibility

was everywhere. The city, Jones
says, was vibrant.

"A lot of bands came out of that
era [the 2010s]," he says. "It's cool
to see the impact that we made
now, the echoes of it today."

Around that time, before his
rise to rock stardom, the six-
string shredder was listening to
artists like Nirvana, Hendrix, and
Soundgarden, trying to decon-
struct their albums in his head
as he prepared to cut his first
with Mix. Considering all this—
the venues, the artist lineage,
the proximity to the tools for
recording—it would seem that
Jones is correct: Seattle is an
abundant proving ground with
all the necessary equipment and
elements to foster a career. In
every neighborhood, there are
places to showcase your sound.
The city is a living, breathing
master class for the aspiring
artist, with teachers like Mix,
Ben Gibbard, Nancy Wilson, and
McCready generously offering
their insight and advice. "The
community," says Jones, "really
supports itself here."

▲ Fans enjoy the return of Bumbershoot music festival, Seattle, 2023

LEFT AT LONDON

SINGLE: "MY FRIENDS ARE KINDA STRANGE"

RECORD: TRANSGENDER
STREET LEGEND, VOL. 2

RELEASED: 2020 | **RECORDED IN:** SEATTLE

PRODUCER: DYLAN BRADY, NAT PUFF

LABEL: SELF-RELEASED

Seattle's Left at London, also known as Nat Puff, began to gain attention in the city around 2018, thanks to the keen ears of folks like DJ Marco Collins. As such, Left at London landed on a number of local experts' year-end lists that called out her sticky track, "Revolution Lover," from the album *Transgender Street Legend, Vol. 1*. The song swells with strings and booms on the low-end with a deep piano beat.

In interviews with outlets like Artist Home, itself a crucial local music resource, the artist talked about growing up influenced by hip-hop and specifically the genre's percussive elements. She was introduced to the sounds by her sister, a dance teacher. These days, Left at London often sings on her tracks in falsetto, bringing a pop

quality to the arrangements. Employing
both lo-fi and high-end production
styles, Left at London has released
a number of albums to date, including
Transgender Street Legend, Vol. 2 and
Vol. 3.

On *Vol. 2*, the song "My Friends Are
Kinda Strange" incorporates harmonies
that recall gospel choirs and would
feel right at home on top-40 radio.
Today, Left at London enjoys a large
social media following and a rabid
audience. She's also constantly producing new work, if not music, then comedy, poetry, or internet videos (she
garnered attention early in her career
for parody videos of artists like Frank
Ocean and Tyler, the Creator). Other
catchy songs from the songwriter's
catalog include "Felt Like I Had Died"
and "Do You See Us? (feat. Nobi)."
With praise from *Forbes*, *Vice*, and
Billboard, Left at London is not only
an important part of the Seattle sound,
she's also an artist on the rise and on
the move.

LIL MOSEY

SINGLE: "BLUEBERRY FAYGO"

RECORD: CERTIFIED HITMAKER (REISSUE)

RELEASED: 2020 | **RECORDED IN:** SEATTLE

PRODUCER: ROYCE DAVID | **LABEL:** INTERSCOPE

Throughout the history of Seattle music, many big-name artists have made important sonic contributions. But while the region has a great deal of art and authenticity, it can be rare to find an artist who appeals to the masses in such a way like rapper and singer Lil Mosey. The young songwriter—still in his early twenties as of this book's writing—was born in Mountlake Terrace, Washington and was raised in the north end of the city, rising to mass popularity in 2017 while still a teenager.

The internet has become a viable way for an artist to make a name in music and Lil Mosey (born Lathan Moses Stanley Echols) has done just that. His first hit was the 2017 song "Pull Up." And that was followed by several other tracks, which have garnered millions of eyes and ears. But it's his song "Blueberry Faygo," which has garnered *hundreds* of millions of plays on YouTube alone, that has made Mosey a music celebrity thanks to its catchy auto-tuned delivery and irreverence.

The song, which was leaked
on Spotify in 2019 ahead of
its formal release, garnered
millions of plays even before
Mosey dropped it officially
months later. It was a high
watermark for the songwriter, but a lower
moment came in 2021: he was accused of rape.
After taking and passing two lie-detector tests
administered by the police, the trial began in
late February 2023 and ten days later, Mosey was
found not guilty.

The songwriter, who boasts four million
Instagram followers, has already started
working on and releasing new music. It
would seem that the blueberry Faygo-
colored sky is the only limit.

DEEP SEA DIVER

SINGLE: "IMPOSSIBLE WEIGHT"

RECORD: IMPOSSIBLE WEIGHT

RELEASED: 2020 | **RECORDED IN:** SEATTLE

PRODUCER: ANDY D. PARK, JESSICA DOBSON | **LABEL:** ATO RECORDS

In Seattle, stars walk among us. Case in point: Jessica Dobson, the mild-mannered guitar master who has performed with artists like Conor Oberst, Yeah Yeah Yeahs, the Shins, and Beck. (Fun fact: Beck lived in the PNW for a short time and recorded with Calvin Johnson and K Records in the early '90s. He also has family in the area.) Impressive stuff. Dobson was even signed to Atlantic Records at just nineteen. But it's with her own band, Deep Sea Diver, which she started with her husband and drummer Peter Mansen, in which she's fully thrown herself.

The group, rounded out with Elliot Jackson and Garrett Gue, released their debut EP in 2009 and their debut LP *History Speaks* in 2012. (Dobson was touring with the Shins at the time.) But it was the band's 2020 LP, released on the Dave Matthews-founded label ATO Records, that led to their breakthrough. The album's self-titled lead single features iconic indie rocker Sharon Van Etten and garnered Deep Sea Diver and its brilliant frontwoman more attention. But, as Dobson notes on the album, this can be a curse, an *impossible weight*.

It was a perfect song to come out during a very
imperfect time, the COVID-19 pandemic. Everything
felt like an impossible weight to bear, from the
virus to the racial injustices and subsequent protests. But Deep Sea Diver showed listeners that
there was at least a modicum of triumph in working, creating more music. Art is sometimes the
only way to shoulder the burden. And Dobson, ever
the bright light, reminded us of this during a
very dark time.

AYRON JONES

SINGLE: "MERCY"

RECORD: CHILD OF THE STATE

RELEASED: 2021 | **RECORDED IN:** SEATTLE

PRODUCER: JOHN VARVATOS, SCOTT BORCHETTA

LABEL: BIG MACHINE RECORDS

It was almost a normal night like any other in 2012. People were at a local dive, waiting to hear live music. But when the singer/lead guitarist started on stage, he did something unexpected halfway through one song. He went to the back of the venue and ordered a drink at the bar . . . while still playing his guitar solo. The bartender gave him his drink and the singer/lead guitarist headed back to the stage and finished the song. Who the hell was this guy?

Ayron Jones, that's who, the latest Seattle rocker to hit No. 1 on the Billboard Mainstream Rock Airplay chart (and one of the few Black artists to do so). Jones, who recorded his debut solo album with Seattle music legend Sir Mix-a-Lot, could well be the future of rock. Mix even said so, after seeing Jones order the drink mid-solo.

Born in 1986 in Seattle, Jones paid his dues on his way up, performing in myriad local venues to mostly empty rooms. He's now performing to tens

of thousands on tour, sharing stages with some
of the biggest bands in the business, from the
Rolling Stones to Guns N' Roses, Janelle Monáe,
Jeff Beck, Public Enemy, and many more.

Jones started his first band Ayron Jones and the
Way in 2010. Fast forward to 2020 and he signed
with Big Machine/John Varvatos and released
his first single, "Take Me Away." The following
year he released "Mercy." Both songs were part
of his first major label release, *Child of the
State*, which dropped in 2021 and includes some
production work from the Screaming Trees'
Barrett Martin. The record's title highlights the
early years of Jones's life, a time when he was
abandoned by his parents at seven years old. He
was adopted by his aunt, who exposed the young
Jones to gospel and soul music. "Mercy" is as
meaningful as it is sonically heavy, pointing to
the racial unrest of 2020 and 2021 and calling
out inequality in the United States. The song hit
No. 1 on the Billboard rock chart, pointing the
way for the future of rock and Jones's career.

LONDON BRIDGE STUDIO

**20021 BALLINGER WAY NE
SUITE A, SHORELINE**

In their teen years, brothers Raj and Rakesh "Rick" Parashar began their musical journey recording in their basement. That lasted until 1985 when they opened the 5,000-square-foot facility known today as London Bridge Studio. Utilizing the space, Rick not only produced some of the best-known songs and albums from this era, but he was also a percussionist and piano and organ player, and he played on several tracks by the iconic artists he recorded, including those from Temple of the Dog and Pearl Jam.

In August of 2014, Rick Parashar passed away at fifty. But together, the Parashar brothers' work has had a powerful impact when it comes to the sound of Seattle during the late '80s and into the '90s. London Bridge was responsible for a host of albums and bands that broke through. Those who have recorded in the famed studio include Alice in Chains, Blind Melon, Pearl Jam, Temple of the Dog, 3 Doors Down, Soundgarden, Screaming Trees, Mother Love Bone, Melissa Etheridge, Queensrÿche, and Dave Matthews. And more recent hitmakers include Brandi Carlile, Fleet Foxes, Ayron Jones, and Macklemore & Ryan Lewis.

London Bridge Studio, located on Ballinger Way Northeast in Shoreline, Washington, is currently owned and operated by record producers Eric Lilavois, Geoff Ott, and Jonathan Plum, who together have produced about a dozen albums and singles that have since gone platinum and/or landed on the Billboard charts, including most recently Jones' LP *Child of the State*. To record, the studio—one of several iconic hubs which include Sound House and Robert Lang Studios— uses a vintage Neve 8048 that's been onsite since 1985 and has since been restored. This "oldie but goodie" gives the studio just one of its unique selling points.

London Bridge not only contributes to the culture that is the Seattle sound, but in many ways it pioneered it, from its early days of grunge through Macklemore & Ryan Lewis. Indeed, *this* London Bridge is not made up of mere wood and wires, but of gold and platinum records that line the walls of the studio's lobby.

BLIMES AND GAB

SINGLE: "SHELLYS (IT'S CHILL)"

RECORD: TALK ABOUT IT

RELEASED: 2020 | **RECORDED IN:** LOS ANGELES

PRODUCER: LOUALLDAY, CAMBO MUSIC, THE ROSWELL UNIVERSE

LABEL: SONY ORCHARD

For rappers Gifted Gab and Blimes Brixton, the 2018 song "Come Correct" opened a lot of doors. The two lyricists knew each other from music circles and the internet as early as 2016, but they met up in Seattle in 2018 and decided to collaborate on the song. Their world exploded. Suddenly, their online video went viral and garnered millions of views. Then they re-recorded the track in earnest and earned another two-million-plus streams on YouTube alone.

The two-minute "Come Correct" displays the rappers' snarly, savvy, and rich lexicon. Both are lyricists in the purest form. If mumble rap and lavishly produced hip-hop have worn thin, San Francisco's Blimes and Seattle's Gab offer up a welcome alternative: a classic New York City underground style where wordplay and cunning are prized. The duo, who have worked with the likes of Method Man and Atmosphere, followed up their success with an LP in 2020, *Talk About It*, for which they garnered even more attention and critical praise, fielding interviews from the likes of Grammy.com and *Billboard*. The duo's song "Feelin It" was also featured in the HBO television series *Insecure*.

The lead single from *Talk About It* was the buoyant 2020 track, "Shellys (It's Chill)." And the accompanying music video features an '80s- and '90s-inspired array of DeLorean cars, early computer graphics, a T. rex, and Gab dressed as former Seattleite and television fortune teller Miss Cleo.

But the star of Blimes and Gabs' show is always the lyrics. This fundamental skill will never go out of style. Fads may come and go, but pure lyricism, rhymes, and vocabulary never will.

BLACK BELT EAGLE SCOUT

SINGLE: "MY BLOOD RUNS THROUGH THIS LAND"

RECORD: THE LAND, THE WATER, THE SKY

RELEASED: 2023 | **RECORDED IN:** ANACORTES, WA

PRODUCER: KATHERINE PAUL, TAKIAYA REED | **LABEL:** SADDLE CREEK

Katherine Paul, the frontwoman of the Pacific Northwest-based band Black Belt Eagle Scout, first found herself face-to-face with a guitar while on a trip to Guatemala with her anthropologist mother. It was a handmade classical and it was soon hers. Later, as a teenager in the Northwest, Paul fell for bands like Nirvana. She would watch VHS tapes, studying Kurt Cobain's hands, learning how to play like him.

Paul has released three studio LPs and one EP since she started the Black Belt Eagle Scout project in 2014. Speaking about her 2023 album and its single, "My Blood Runs Through This Land," Paul said the way she recorded the guitar is meant to emulate who she is as a person. The song is rich with intense riffs gilded with at times hectic tremolo. On the song, she layers distorted electrics in a way that makes you feel as if you're rushing by your surroundings on the way toward *something*. As if you're chasing freedom.

For years, Paul was based in Portland, Oregon. But more recently the artist relocated back to where she grew up: the Swinomish Indian Tribal Community in Washington. That's also where she wrote her 2023 LP, observing the surrounding nature and channeling it through the music, especially her guitar. Paul's music has also recently been featured on the popular television show, *Reservation Dogs*. With each passing day, she becomes more of a force.

KASSA OVERALL

SINGLE: "GOING UP"

RECORD: ANIMALS

RELEASED: 2023 | **RECORDED IN:** SEATTLE; NEW YORK CITY; OAKLAND, CA

PRODUCER: KASSA OVERALL, LAUREN DU GRAFE | **LABEL:** WARP RECORDS

Most kids growing up get their big siblings'
clothing hand-me-downs. And if they're lucky,
maybe their sports trading card collection.
But for Kassa Overall, he only had eyes for his
big brother Carlos's drum kit. Overall, who
was already banging on the drums as a toddler,
attended Seattle's renowned Garfield High School
(past grads include Jimi Hendrix, Philip Woo,
and Quincy Jones). He then went on to study
percussion at the Oberlin Conservatory
of Music before settling in Brooklyn,
New York.

More recently, in his professional career,
Overall has worked and collaborated with
many musical big names, including Yoko Ono,
Jon Batiste, and Das Racist. Overall's music
touches on real life experiences, such as
his struggles with mental health. While he has
talked openly about spending time in an insti-
tution battling manic episodes during his
early life, Overall's music later became a
safe space to further explore, share, and
confront these issues. His 2023 album,

ANIMALS, which features production from artists like Jherek Bischoff (a former Seattle-based artist who's worked with musicians like David Byrne), explores realities outside of his personal experience. It highlights themes of human behavior in so-called civilized societies that in practice may not be quite so civilized. It was also recognized by the *New York Times* as a top 3 jazz album of 2023

"Going Up" features local standouts Shabazz Palaces, Lil B, and Francis and the Lights, and centers around the cost of connection, the loss that sometimes stems from love, and what people take with them after a romance ends. The song is also hopeful, hinting at the chance of a new future. Today, Overall is part of a new wave of musicians bridging the already historically connected genres of jazz and hip-hop. He is a wizard, and his spells are mind-opening musical gifts.

CONCLUSION

Seattle and its surrounding areas provide beautiful views, proximity to nature, and fertile ground for creative experimentation. Whether it's the constant rain pushing people indoors or the vibrant communities that rise up from such a rich, artistic atmosphere, the region has long been a place people travel to and put down roots in order to discover both music and themselves.

In this way, Seattle is a place for people to grow. Just like the lush, verdant flora that eagerly blossoms in the PNW during the spring and summer months, the city's creative force is afforded a great deal of room to try new things, to grow and bloom. It's this reality that helped spawn strange though masterful songs about barracudas, big butts, Teen Spirit deodorant, and thrift shopping.

It's because of this vibe that whole new genres can come forth, from grunge to smooth jazz. The city is a place where, if you introduce yourself as someone in a band, you're earnestly taken seriously. Seattleites might take this for granted, but it isn't like this everywhere else. But Seattle and its people respect those who try to further the region's musical legacy. It's as important here as the air we breathe.

We hope you've enjoyed this journey through 101 songs and the many more musicians who brought them to life. In truth, there were more we would have liked to highlight, but perhaps that will be for another time and tome. In the meantime, we would like to tip our proverbial caps to the artists who appear in these pages.

You are eternal.

ACKNOWLEDGMENTS

We would like to thank our families. Work like this would be significantly less worthwhile without them to share it with. We would also like to thank our friends at Sasquatch Books, including Jen Worick and Alison Keefe, and everyone else who had a hand in this production. Finally, we would like to thank Seattle itself, and the creative home it's offered countless musicians these many decades. The city's music scene, vibrant and diverse, brought the authors together, including in marriage. And we hope this book reflects our gratitude and honors the area for its impact on our lives. Thank you, as always, for reading.

Special thanks to Gaynell Walker, Cedric David, Olivia Walker, Michelle Freeman, David Uitti, Susie Uitti, Jane Uitti, Luke Uitti, Libby Uitti, Robb Benson, Caleb Thompson, Alaia D'Alessandro, Morgan Chosnyk, Julia Massey, Dominic and Jared Cortese, and all the people we're lucky to have in our lives. Thanks also to Merrilee Rush, Nancy Wilson, Jack Endino, Sir Mix-a-Lot, Ben Gibbard, Mary Lambert, and Ayron Jones for their time and expertise.

FURTHER READING

Jackson Street After Hours: The Roots of Jazz in Seattle
by Paul De Barros, Sasquatch Books (1993)

Encyclopedia of Northwest Music by James Bush,
Sasquatch Books (1999)

Heavier Than Heaven: A Biography of Kurt Cobain
by Charles R. Cross, Hachette Books (2001)

Room Full of Mirrors: A Biography of Jimi Hendrix
by Charles R. Cross, Hachette Books (2005)

*Love Rock Revolution: K Records and the Rise of Independent
Music* by Mark Baumgarten, Sasquatch Books (2012)

Kicking & Dreaming: A Story of Heart, Soul, and Rock and Roll
by Ann Wilson, Nancy Wilson, and Charles R. Cross, It Books
(2012)

Everybody Loves Our Town: An Oral History of Grunge
by Mark Yarm, Crown (2012)

Total F*cking Godhead: The Biography of Chris Cornell
by Corbin Reiff, Post Hill Press (2020)

Emerald Street: A History of Hip Hop in Seattle
by Daudi Abe, University of Washington Press (2020)

The Storyteller: Tales of Life and Music by Dave Grohl,
Dey Street Books (2021)

Broken Horses: A Memoir by Brandi Carlile, Crown (2022)

INDEX

IMAGE CREDITS

Front cover: Comet Tavern image reprinted with permssion from Jason Lajeunesse; © alexincaliphoto/ AdobeStock (guitar); © Veniamin Kraskov/ AdobeStock (coat); © timonko/Adobe Stock (tag); © Eric Skadson/ Adobe Stock (No Vacancy sign); "The Electric Lady Studio Guitar" sculpture by Daryl Smith permission by Michael Malone, Hunters Capital; © vachcameraman/ Adobe Stock (drum kit); © pio3/Adobe Stock (angel)

Back cover: Showbox drawing by Alison Keefe based on image reprinted with permission of Shannon Welles; Carrie Brownstein by Andy Witchger (see page 151 for full credit); © Miguel Garcia Saaved/Adobe Stock (trumpet)

vii, 6, 10, 24, 30, 44, 50, 66, 76, 80, 106, 112, 168, 236, 262, and 287: Original drawings by Alison Keefe

ii: © Tim Fleming/Alamy Stock Photo

x: Marquee at Showbox Theater on 1st Ave., Seattle, 1940. MOHAI, Al Smith Collection, 2014.49.006-027-0073

5: © Silvio/Adobe Stock; © SunwArt/Adobe Stock

9: Ray Charles in der Hamburger Musikhalle, September 1971 by Heinrich Klaffs (https://flickr.com/photos/47686431@N04/4505892467) is licensed under CC-BY-SA. Color and crop modified from original.

13: Image reprinted with permission of Alison Keefe

15: © AGCuesta/Adobe Stock

18–19: Paul Revere and the Raiders at a press conference in Seattle, 1967 (Dave Potts, photographer). MOHAI, *Seattle Post-Intelligencer* Collection, 1986.5.38441

21: 1965 promotional image of Loretta Lynn by Les Leverett (https://www.gannett-cdn.com/media/Nashville/Nashville/2014/04/11//1397259219003-DN-20100121-TUNEIN-1210808-4.jpg?width=1184&format=pjpg&auto=webp&quality=100) is licensed under CC-BY-SA. Color and crop modified from original.

22–23: Dave Lewis onstage by Panorama Records, Seattle, Washington, ca. 1966. HistoryLink.org. https://www.historylink.org/File/8684

27: © ink drop/Adobe Stock

28-29: © elephotos/Adobe Stock

33: © pio3/Adobe Stock

37: Item 77472, Bumbershoot Festival Records (Record Series 5807-05), Seattle Municipal Archives.

40: © Morena/Adobe Stock

42–43: Endless winding piano keys render from https://pixy.org/4363106 is licensed by CC BY-NC-ND 4.0.

43: © venusangel/Adobe Stock

48–49: Nancy Wilson and Roger Fisher of the American rock band Heart by Jim Summaria (http://www.jimsummariaphoto.com) is licensed under CC-BY-SA. Color and crop modified from original.

56–57: © nerthuz/Adobe Stock

58: © Morena/Adobe Stock

61: © jordano/Adobe Stock

63: © pixelrobot/Adobe Stock; © abidika/Adobe Stock

64: Image reprinted with permission by Cyndia Michelle Lavik

69: © Roman Tiraspolsky/Adobe Stock

71: © fergregory/Adobe Stock; © Olga Moonlight/Adobe Stock

72–73: © Nomad_Soul/Adobe Stock

75: © Dmitri Krasovski/Adobe Stock

79: © Jo Ann Snover/Adobe Stock

82–83: © Daria/Adobe Stock

87: Nirvana performing during MTV taping at Pier 48, Seattle, December 13, 1993, MOHAI, *Seattle Post-Intelligencer Collection*, 2000.107.132.29.02

88–89: © panigystovska/Adobe Stock

90–91: © kamil/Adobe Stock

93: © BillionPhotos.com/Adobe Stock

94–95: © Zamrznuti tonovi/Adobe Stock

96–97: Image reprinted with permission of David Hawkes

99: © Eagle/Adobe Stock

101: © Punkbarby/Adobe Stock

102–103: © sangsiripech/Adobe Stock

104–105: © Shapla/Adobe Stock

105: © Rysak/Adobe Stock (background); © Yevhen/Adobe Stock (anarchy symbol); © Addison Spates/Adobe Stock (pom poms)

107–109: Love Battery, a band from Seattle, Washington, USA performing at the Mural Amphitheatre, Seattle Center by Joe Mabel (https://commons.wikimedia.org/wiki/User:Jmabel) is licensed under CC-BY-SA. Color and crop modified from original.

111: © Marcela Ruty Romero/Adobe Stock

114–115: © Piotr Krzeslak/Adobe Stock

117: American rock band Alice in Chains in a promo photo by Paul Hernandez (*City Heat* Magazine, December 1988) is licensed under CC-BY-SA.

119: © Music Instruments/Adobe Stock

121: Mudhoney 01 Manchester International 1 1st December 1989 by Paul Blackwood (https://commons.wikimedia.org/wiki/File:Mudhoney_01_Manchester_International_1_1st_December_1989.jpg) is licensed under CC-BY-SA. Color is modified from original.

123: Seattle, WA (2022) by Another Believer (https://commons.wikimedia.org/wiki/User:Another_Believer) is licensed under CC-BY-SA. Color is modified from original. Comet Tavern image reprinted with permssion from Jason Lajeunesse.

125: © Supplied By Globe Photos, Inc/Globe Photos/ ZUMAPRESS.com

127: © taffpixture/Adobe Stock; © mode_list/Adobe Stock

129: Buzz Osborne The Melvins Live @ Slim's 03 by Peter Alfred Hess (https://www.flickr.com/photos/22799676@N03/5018472217) is licensed under CC-BY-SA. Color is modified from original.

130–131: BikiniKBrixt110619-25 by Raph_PH (https://www.flickr.com/photos/raph_ph/48986068321/) is licensed under CC-BY-SA. Color and crop modified from original.

132: © Morena/Adobe Stock

135: Chris Cornell at Bilbao BBK Live 2009 by Alberto Cabello (https://www.flickr.com/photos/pixel-illo/4935398434/) is licensed under CC-BY-SA. Color is modified from original.

137: © Jim Palmer/Adobe Stock

138–139: © Jongchun/Adobe Stock

140–141: © cobracz/Adobe Stock
143: © Oner/Adobe Stock
144–145: © Eric Laudonien/Adobe Stock
147: © Denis Rozhnovsky/Adobe Stock
151: Carrie Brownstein - Sleater Kinney - Palace Theatre - St. Paul, Minnesota by Andy Witchger (https://www.flickr.com/photos/42878734@N06/48988110742/) is licensed under CC-BY-SA. Color and crop modified from original.
153: © rostyle/Adobe Stock
155: Dave Grohl by Roger Woolman (https://commons.wikimedia.org/wiki/File:Dave_Grohl_(132997591).jpeg) is licensed under CC-BY-SA. Color and crop modified from the original.
157: © BreizhAtao/Adobe Stock (flag); Sean Nelson of Harvey Danger © WENN Rights Ltd/Alamy Stock Photo
159: Reggie Watts performing at Punkt 2012 by Jørund Føreland Pedersen (https://commons.wikimedia.org/wiki/User:Joerundfp) is licensed under CC-BY-SA. Color and crop modified from original.
163: Crocodile Cafe by Chris Brown (https://www.flickr.com/photos/zoonabar/530433689/) is licensed under CC-BY-SA. Color and crop modified from original.
165: Pedro The Lion in 2017 by Bob Andrews (https://commons.wikimedia.org/wiki/File:Pedro-The-Lion-2017.jpg) is licensed under CC-BY-SA. Color and crop modified from original.
167: © karagrubis/Adobe Stock
171: The Blood Brothers performing live at the Capitol Hill Block Party on July 27, 2007 by Alex Blackstock (https://www.flickr.com/photos/17456820@N00/927565672) is licensed under CC-BY-SA. Color and crop modified from original.
173: Police Car Amarillo by by Tony Hisgett (https://www.flickr.com/photos/hisgett/15392677526/) is licensed under CC-BY-SA. Color and crop modified from original.
175: © Eric Skadson/Adobe Stock
178–179: Neko Case by David Lee (https://www.flickr.com/photos/davidjlee/28759198148/) is licensed under CC-BY-SA. Color and crop modified from original.
181: © MuhammadFadhli/Adobe Stock
182–183: © WorldFoto/Alamy Stock Photo
185: © Train arrival/Adobe Stock
186–187: © wojtek/Adobe Stock
190–191: Dave Matthews performing with the Dave Matthews Band at the Outside Lands 2009 by Moses (https://www.flickr.com/photos/36416130@N03/3873194961/) is licensed under CC-BY-SA. Color and crop modified from original.
195: Image reprinted with permission by Mike Sampson
196–197: © Hotte Pics/Adobe Stock
198–199: The Head and the Heart by Afunk45 (https://commons.wikimedia.org/wiki/File:THATH_sunset.jpg) is licensed under CC-BY-SA. Color and crop modified from original.
200–201: Image reprinted with permission of Renata Steiner/KEXP
202: © Morena/Adobe Stock
204–205: © kanpisut/Adobe Stock; © indigolotos/Adobe Stock
207: Seattle rapper Sol performing at Neumos, Capitol Hill, Seattle, Washington by Joe Mabel (https://commons.wikimedia.org/wiki/File:Sol_(Seattle_rapper)_02.jpg) is licensed under CC-BY-SA. Color and crop modified from original.
209: Image reprinted with permission from Stasia Irons and SassyBlack/Subpop Records
211: Allen Stone performing at the Chataqua festival in Chewelah, Washington by Baronem (https://commons.wikimedia.org/wiki/File:Allen_Stone_at_Chataqua_2013.jpg) is licensed under CC-BY-SA. Color and crop modified from original.
213: © AKGK Studio/Adobe Stock
215: © Veniamin Kraskov/Adobe Stock; © timonko/Adobe Stock
216–217: © New Africa/Adobe Stock
218: © Valeriy Lebedev/Adobe Stock
219: © Miguel Garcia Saaved/Adobe Stock
221: Damien_Jurado-2 by Abby Gillardi (https://www.flickr.com/photos/abbers13/16587076082/)) is licensed under CC-BY-SA. Color and crop modified from original.
222–223: © ON-Photography/Adobe Stock
224–225: © SevenThreeSky/Adobe Stock; ©nys/Adobe Stock; © fotofabrika/Adobe Stock
226–227: Perfume Genius @ The Independent by Allan Wan (https://www.flickr.com/photos/critter-spun/15656661892/) is licensed under CC-BY-SA. Color and crop modified from original.
229: Image reprinted with permission of Shervin Lainez
230–231: © tsuguliev/Adobe Stock
232–233: © itim2101/Adobe Stock
235: Brandi Carlile walks the red carpet at the 2023 Gershwin Prize for Popular Song Concert by Library of Congress Life (https://www.flickr.com/photos/library-of-congress-life/52723752056/) is licensed under CC-BY-SA. Color modified from original.
239: Image reprinted with permission of Alley Rutzel
240–241: Car Seat Headrest @ The Sinclair by Kenny Sun (https://www.flickr.com/photos/kenny-ysun/29129739303/) is licensed under CC-BY-SA. Color and crop modified from original.
243: © Bert-Jan/Adobe Stock
244–245: © evmarya/Adobe Stock
247: © JP Photography/Adobe Stock
249: Travis Thompson in LA Studio by Erick.merc (https://commons.wikimedia.org/wiki/File:Travis_Thompson.jpg) is licensed under CC-BY-SA. Color and crop modified from original.
253: © james anderson/Alamy Stock Photo
257: Lil Mosey by The Come Up Show (https://www.flickr.com/photos/thecomeupshow/41879461061/) is licensed under CC-BY-SA. Color and crop modified from original
257: Faygo image reprinted with permission from Max Lovalvo
258-259: Deep Sea Diver by David Lee (https://www.flickr.com/photos/davidjlee/27582390121/) is licensed under CC-BY-SA. Color and crop modified from original.
261: Image reprinted with permission of Karen Mason Blair
265: Image reprinted with permission of Dolly Ave
266–267: SXSW 2019 - Black Belt Eagle Scout by Paul Hudson (https://www.flickr.com/photos/pahud-son/47359174041/) is licensed under CC-BY-SA. Color and crop modified from original.
269: © Artranq/Adobe Stock

EVA WALKER is a DJ and radio host at KEXP 90.3 FM. Born and raised in Seattle, Eva cofounded the popular rock band The Black Tones with her twin brother, Cedric. Together they've shared stages with Weezer, Death Cab for Cutie, and Mavis Staples, and have collaborated with Pearl Jam's Mike McCready. On their music journey, the band has shown a city the value of family.

JAKE UITTI is a writer based in Seattle. His work has been featured in the *Guardian*, *Interview*, *Vanity Fair*, and *American Songwriter*. He also coauthored memoirs with former NBA standouts Muggsy Bogues and Earl Cureton. This is his second book with Sasquatch.